Programming for PaaS

Lucas Carlson

Beijing · Cambridge · Farnham · Köln · Sebastopol · Tokyo

Programming for PaaS

by Lucas Carlson

Copyright © 2013 Lucas Carlson. All rights reserved.

Printed in the United States of America.

Published by O'Reilly Media, Inc., 1005 Gravenstein Highway North, Sebastopol, CA 95472.

O'Reilly books may be purchased for educational, business, or sales promotional use. Online editions are also available for most titles (*http://my.safaribooksonline.com*). For more information, contact our corporate/institutional sales department: 800-998-9938 or *corporate@oreilly.com*.

Editors: Mike Loukides and Meghan Blanchette
Production Editor: Kara Ebrahim
Copyeditor: Jasmine Kwityn
Proofreader: Rachel Head

Indexer: Lucie Haskins
Cover Designer: Randy Comer
Interior Designer: David Futato
Illustrator: Rebecca Demarest

August 2013:   First Edition

Revision History for the First Edition:

2013-07-22:   First release

2014-04-04:   Second release

2014-05-08:   Third release

See *http://oreilly.com/catalog/errata.csp?isbn=9781449334901* for release details.

ISBN: 978-1-449-33490-1

[LSI]

For Yoscelina, My Love,

Thank you for every nano-amount of support. I honestly do not think this book would be here if it were not for you and your encouragement. I love you for everything.

—Lucas Carlson

Table of Contents

Preface

Programming Is Hard

Programming is a hard job. Deceivingly so. At first you write code, and it works, and you are happy. Then it has bugs and you spend hours, days, even weeks trying to find, fix, and resolve bugs and edge cases. Then when you have everything perfectly programmed and just when you thought the job couldn't get harder, you have to go deploy your code. *vim apache.conf. vim my.cnf. vim /etc/hosts. iptables.* Just when you thought you were a programmer, all of a sudden you get waist deep in system administration and wonder how you got there.

If there is one thing that programmers are good at, it is being productively lazy. When a programmer does the same thing over and over again, eventually he thinks: can't my computer do this for me? Around 2005, enough programmers in the world had edited *apache.conf* files that something dramatically changed. A few brilliant programmers decided they didn't want to do it any more.

Out of this came two paradigms that have forever changed the landscape of deploying applications in the world: DevOps and PaaS. DevOps's response to *apache.conf* editing says: I can write code templates (called recipes or cookbooks) that do system administration for me. PaaS's response to *apache.conf* editing says: I can write a program that manages system administration for me. Many great books have been written about DevOps—like *Puppet Types and Providers* by Dan Bode and Nan Liu or *Test-Driven Infrastructure with Chef* by Stephen Nelson-Smith—but few books have been written about PaaS.

PaaS is great because you get the benefits of dedicated hosting (like each app running in its own process and load balanced to scale) with the ease of shared hosting (you don't do any configuration management, the PaaS does it for you). But those benefits come at a cost. You have to write code that works with the PaaS.

Writing Code That Works on PaaS

This topic has not been written about a lot: *which programming patterns work well on PaaS and which anti-patterns no longer work in a PaaS environment?* This is the entire theme of this book. Although the popularity of PaaS has grown exponentially with millions of developers worldwide having already adopted it and millions more starting to learn about it right now, not a lot of work has been written to help guide developers on how to successfully incorporate PaaS best practices into their coding processes.

Specifically, one of the biggest challenges facing many developers working in businesses today is how to move legacy code and older applications into a PaaS paradigm. There have been few resources to help guide people through this challenge and hopefully this book will be a first step in the right direction to providing the dialogue.

Audience

This book is aimed at programmers, developers, engineers, and architects who want to know more about Platform-as-a-Service.

You do not need to be a programmer to find value in this book. In fact, if you are trying to convince your boss to let you use PaaS inside your company, you may want to give your boss a copy of this book. Alternatively, you can find resources for talking to your boss about PaaS, both the pros and cons, in Chapter 8. This will show you have thought through the problem from both sides of the table and have an informed opinion, not just a passing fashion.

In some of the technical chapters, I even provide code samples. Since PaaS works with many programming languages, I provided simple programming samples in various programming languages including PHP, Ruby, Node.js, Java, and Objective-C. We do not go deep in any one language, but rather stay high level on various ones in hopes that you are familiar with one or two and can read through the others.

The Structure of This Book

If you are an architect or technical manager, or are simply new to PaaS, the first three chapters are very important to understand the context for which PaaS has entered the technical landscape. These chapters explain what the cloud is (Chapter 1), what PaaS is (Chapter 2), and different kinds of PaaS technologies and their relative strengths and weaknesses (Chapter 3).

If you already know about the history of PaaS or have used a PaaS, you can skim through the first three chapters and dig in for the next three chapters around Chapters 4, 5, or 6. These chapters are the heart of this book, providing real life tools, techniques, and programming patterns that will help you stay away from the biggest pitfalls of PaaS and not waste any time on programming anti-patterns.

Chapter 7 is an important chapter for everyone to understand. Services like database and caching services or email services contain some of the biggest gotchas in the PaaS world. If you are not careful, this is the place you can fail most quickly when adopting PaaS.

The next two chapters go back to a higher level of understanding. In Chapter 8, there is discussion around the appropriateness of adopting PaaS at all, including the strengths and weaknesses of PaaS in general. Understanding whether PaaS is a good fit for the problem you are tackling is critical. In Chapter 9, the discussion centers around where PaaS is going, some industry trends, and thoughts around Open Source movements in the PaaS world.

The last chapter is a great place to reference any technologies available around PaaS. Chapter 10 should have a bookmark sticking out of it, because you will be flipping to it to find ideas for service providers and technologies of all types (PaaS, IaaS, SaaS, and helpful programming libraries).

Conventions Used in This Book

The following typographical conventions are used in this book:

Italic
> Indicates new terms, URLs, email addresses, filenames, and file extensions.

`Constant width`
> Used for program listings, as well as within paragraphs to refer to program elements such as variable or function names, databases, data types, environment variables, statements, and keywords.

`Constant width bold`
> Shows commands or other text that should be typed literally by the user.

`Constant width italic`
> Shows text that should be replaced with user-supplied values or by values determined by context.

 This icon signifies a tip, suggestion, or general note.

This icon indicates a warning or caution.

Safari® Books Online

 Safari Books Online (*www.safaribooksonline.com*) is an on-demand digital library that delivers expert content in both book and video form from the world's leading authors in technology and business.

Technology professionals, software developers, web designers, and business and creative professionals use Safari Books Online as their primary resource for research, problem solving, learning, and certification training.

Safari Books Online offers a range of product mixes and pricing programs for organizations, government agencies, and individuals. Subscribers have access to thousands of books, training videos, and prepublication manuscripts in one fully searchable database from publishers like O'Reilly Media, Prentice Hall Professional, Addison-Wesley Professional, Microsoft Press, Sams, Que, Peachpit Press, Focal Press, Cisco Press, John Wiley & Sons, Syngress, Morgan Kaufmann, IBM Redbooks, Packt, Adobe Press, FT Press, Apress, Manning, New Riders, McGraw-Hill, Jones & Bartlett, Course Technology, and dozens more. For more information about Safari Books Online, please visit us online.

How to Contact Us

Please address comments and questions concerning this book to the publisher:

O'Reilly Media, Inc.
1005 Gravenstein Highway North
Sebastopol, CA 95472
800-998-9938 (in the United States or Canada)
707-829-0515 (international or local)
707-829-0104 (fax)

We have a web page for this book, where we list errata, examples, and any additional information. You can access this page at *http://oreil.ly/programming-paas*.

To comment or ask technical questions about this book, send email to *bookques tions@oreilly.com*.

For more information about our books, courses, conferences, and news, see our website at *http://www.oreilly.com*.

Find us on Facebook: *http://facebook.com/oreilly*

Follow us on Twitter: *http://twitter.com/oreillymedia*

Watch us on YouTube: *http://www.youtube.com/oreillymedia*

Acknowledgments

First, I would like to thank Doug Baldwin for all his assistance putting this book together; it could never have been done without him.

If it were not for Meghan Blanchette's patience and persistence and Mike Loukides believing in me, I would never have started or finished this book.

Thank you to Kara Ebrahim, Meghan Connolly, and the whole O'Reilly crew for making this possible.

This book would be appallingly low quality were it not for our technical reviewers, who spotted bugs, problems, and conceptual errors: John Purrier, Alex Parkinson, Larry Hitchon, Andrei Matei, Chad Keck, and Troy Howard.

To my wife, my son, my daughter, my dog, my mom, my dad, my brother, and all my family and family-in-law, thank you for your everlasting support and love.

Finally, to the programmers and inventors who created PaaS and the companies that supported them, thank you for making all of our lives easier.

CHAPTER 1

The Cloud for Developers

One day, not long ago, Jason Gendron had an idea.

What if he could create a community of Twitter friends, so that instead of just following each other, users might actually have bidirectional communication? Jason, a Chicago-based developer, wrote some code, registered the domain name twitclub.com, and deployed it on a dedicated server. Success was immediate. In a few months, over 80,000 people were using the service. But with success came challenges—the kind of challenges you always say you will be glad to have if only you succeed.

With 80,000 users, Jason was spending half his time handling operations and half his time doing development. He spent less time innovating and more time running the actual app. Before long, hackers compromised his self-configured servers. The hackers sent out terabytes of data, leaving him with an enormous bill. The net result: he was devoting most of his time to battling with servers and not enough to writing code.

Only a few months later, Jason turned to Platform-as-a-Service (PaaS), which allowed him to outsource all the maintenance responsibilities, from software updates to security patches. The benefits were immediately clear. Suddenly he was able to stop thinking about the operations side of his idea, letting his PaaS provider deal with it. That enabled him to spend 100% of his time innovating. Soon he was able to actually quit his day job and devote all his time to his startup, bootstrapping it into a profitable company.

PaaS changed Jason's life, and it can change your life too. It can let you spend more time coding and less time managing servers.

Jason's plight is a familiar one, and its solution—deploying services on PaaS—is one that holds enormous promise, pointing the way toward a future in which cloud-based innovation is drastically easier and much less expensive.

The Developer's Plight

Developers are everywhere. They work in small businesses, in agencies, in enterprises, in startups. All developers are facing the same challenge today: dealing with operations that are coupled with development. The problems may look different depending on your working environment, but the central issue is there nevertheless.

As an example, let's look at the traditional waterfall development process. Typically, the developer works on code and gets it running in a dev/test environment. Then he "throws it over the IT wall," at which point the operations people spend a few weeks to a month getting it quality assured and deployed, creating a huge delay in getting it into production mode. Timelines are delayed. Product testing is delayed. Ultimately, and perhaps most costly, innovation slows down.

Velocity, or the lack thereof, becomes an issue especially with social and mobile applications. You might have a marketing campaign that needs to go up in a hurry and may only last for a few weeks. Going through the typical process of throwing it over the wall could delay you a critical amount of time, especially if there are troubles with the app and you need to make modifications, or if there is simply not enough velocity for today's social market campaigns.

On the other side of the spectrum are developers in small businesses who are simply trying to get their jobs done, and individual developers—innovators like Jason Gendron—who are trying to come up with ideas for the next Instagram or Facebook. PaaS helps them solve the issue of velocity while at the same time providing significant savings by letting them focus on coding.

Looking to the future, these savings promise to have a profound—and very positive—impact on the creation of startups.

What the Cloud Has Done for Innovation

The cloud has transformed how developers create software, speeding up the way developers work around the world, from venture-backed startups all the way to large Fortune 100 corporations.

Modern developers are being asked to do more with less. They are given tight budgets and tighter deadlines to accomplish miraculous feats of development. Cost and convenience have led to widespread adoption of the cloud. The cloud has been the mechanism that lets enterprise developers bypass IT departments and allows entrepreneurs to have access to effectively unlimited-sized data centers without any up-front hardware purchases.

Figure 1-1 tracks venture capital deals over a 10-year period beginning in 2001. It shows normalized data for the total number of deals versus total deal size. As the graph illustrates, the two sets of numbers tracked very closely for several years. Significantly, that changed in 2006, the year Infrastructure-as-a-Service (IaaS) went mainstream when Amazon introduced Amazon Web Services with EC2 and S3. At that point, the cloud decoupled the two trajectories, progressively driving down the deal size and driving up the number of deals.

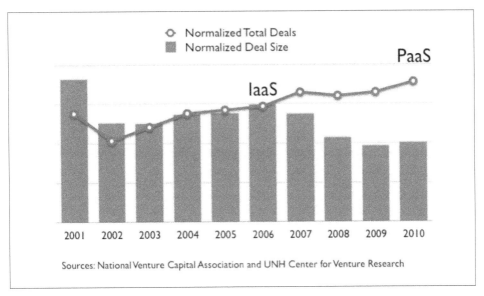

Figure 1-1. Total deal size vs. normalized total deals, 2001–2010

What does this mean? What are the implications?

For the first time in history, there is a decoupling of the total number of deals versus the deal size. By 2010, venture capitalists had to pay only half as much money to fund new companies as they used to. These high-tech companies no longer needed as much capital. They did not need to build out data centers anymore; they could rely on the cloud. That is a key benefit of cloud adoption in venture capital deals.

Through cloud technology like IaaS and PaaS, the 50% cost savings are going to translate into all sorts of business: not just startups and VC-backed companies, but in the mid-market and enterprise worlds as well.

Infrastructure-as-a-Service gets rid of half the problem—the issue of buying and managing data centers. The second half of the problem is managing application operations. Decoupling operations from development is the second and true promise of the cloud, and it's one that Platform-as-a-Service is uniquely poised to deliver.

The Cloud: A Brief History for Programmers

What is the cloud? It is a loaded term and overly used.

Is the cloud just Dropbox? Is it the iPhone? Is it just Gmail?

Maybe for some people these myriad examples are the cloud, but not for a developer.

For a developer, the cloud is a set of foundational technologies built on top of each other to enable new ways of building and running technology. If you can't build a new kind of foundational technology on another foundational technology, it is not the cloud.

Many apps and SaaS are built on foundational cloud technologies. Dropbox and Gmail are SaaS apps built on foundational cloud technology. But they themselves are not cloud technologies.

The 1990s saw the rise of data centers. Third-party companies would put servers into a room and rent them out. This was less expensive than previous constraints, when companies had to buy their own servers and data centers.

With the rise of centralized data servers came virtualization, which represented the first step into the cloud. With virtualization, data centers could consolidate into massive servers subdivided into smaller ("virtualized") servers. VMware and Microsoft were among the early companies to create software that was critical to the development of virtualization.

Introducing APIs

In 2006, on top of virtualization came the next big step into the cloud: the application programming interface (API). APIs added a sophisticated layer of automation, enabling you to control, start, stop, and create new virtual machines through simple and real-time commands. First created by companies such as Amazon with Amazon Web Services, APIs paved the way for Infrastructure-as-a-Service, which heralded a lot of what we now consider cloud standards.

At this point in the history of the cloud, it was so easy to spawn a multitude of virtual machines that managing servers became a headache. With unlimited servers at your fingertips, how do you take care of managing them all? That is where DevOps came into play.

Along Comes DevOps

DevOps became a mainstream force around 2010. It arose from the need of developers to do their jobs faster. They were tired of waiting for operations to deploy their code. They were tired of not having tools to easily manage services. They were tired of having to do it all manually. Out of these frustrations, programmers moved into the cloud and became DevOps gurus. They built systems to manage and maintain infrastructure and to interact with servers in a programmatic fashion.

Important DevOps tools like Chef and Puppet were introduced, providing systems to manage thousands of servers, upgrade code, replace code, replace servers, deploy new servers into a template, and make modifications, all of which had been very labor intensive and difficult from a developer's point of view. We even saw the rise of automated DevOps tools like RightScale and ScaleXtreme.

DevOps offers developers the most control out of all the cloud tools. The trade-off is that you still need to spend time building and managing operations; if things go wrong, you are still the go-to person. And so, DevOps is not the ultimate answer to the hopes of developers. Here's why.

As a developer, you will most likely spend time writing code that works with Chef and Puppet, while your ultimate goal is probably to spend less time managing operations. If that is your goal, Platform-as-a-Service can handle operational tasks for you today, freeing up even more of your time. With PaaS, you do not have to write the Chef cookbooks or the Puppet scripts to manage servers. You can spend more of your time writing the code that interacts with your users.

DevOps technologies were—and remain—essential for application lifecycle management tools, which we'll discuss in a moment. Application lifecycle management would not be possible without DevOps, so DevOps is not going to go away. DevOps is a core foundational technology, and there will always be a need for it in a cloud world.

DevOps tools are also a big part of how any Platform-as-a-Service runs under the covers. For platforms such as Heroku, EngineYard, AppEngine, and AppFog, DevOps tools are essential behind-the-scenes tools.

The Arrival of Application Lifecycle Management

Thanks to DevOps, one can now manage thousands of machines easily, but one still sees the world through the glasses of infrastructure. Applications care more about services (e.g., MySQL and MongoDB) than the details (e.g., what version of *libxml* is installed across virtual machines). Managing services and applications remains outside the grasp of DevOps and even IaaS. The next layer of cloud technology is application lifecycle management.

App lifecycle management tools are typified by technologies like Cloud Foundry, OpenShift, and Cloudify. They are not yet really PaaS (though they sometimes claim to be), because they still need an operator to run them (hence not really removing the big pain of running operations yourself). However, they do provide a cornerstone to PaaS technology. These tools know how to start, stop, and deploy applications. They often know how to run and manage some of your services, like MySQL, as well.

App lifecycle management tools handle applications holistically, managing applications across many different servers, so an application can run on hundreds or even thousands of them. Traditionally, IaaS and DevOps tools have had trouble thinking in terms of applications—of the needs, resources, and services that span hundreds of servers. App lifecycle management understands applications, treats them from a services point of view, and knows how to manage, scale, and maintain them.

In many cases, you can run app lifecycle management tools on your own laptop. Cloud Foundry has a Micro VM that can do a proof of concept very quickly. OpenShift and Cloudify have similar tools. Taking app lifecycle management to the next level and building out a production-ready version of the same tool can be daunting; it often takes teams of 5–10 operations people and involves managing dozens or hundreds of machines, even for small production installations.

The benefits of app lifecycle management are great, though. Take, for example, a Drupal website that is going to be hit by massive traffic overnight. In this example, you'll need to go from a single server to 1,000 servers to handle this huge influx of new users.

Before app lifecycle management, you would need to engage a team to manually figure out how to incorporate hundreds of new servers into the process. You would need to deploy the right code and take a very hands-on approach. It required significant human intervention and it needed to scale with human resources.

Even with DevOps, this can be a daunting task. How do you ensure that the servers that Puppet created are all working the way you expect them to? How do you maintain these servers? How can you see in real time how the application loads are affecting each server? These are only some of the shortcomings of DevOps tools.

An app lifecycle management tool such as Cloud Foundry changes all this. You can tell it that your application needs 1,000 more instances, and Cloud Foundry will do all the plumbing. It makes the changes necessary to run those applications across your servers. It greatly simplifies the process.

But there's a hitch. You still need people watching and monitoring the app lifecycle tool itself. You don't get rid of operations; you are simply shifting your attention from an individual application to the running of your lifecycle tool.

In our example, prior to the advent of app lifecycle management tools, when you needed to scale up the number of servers the development team would interact directly with the operations team to ensure success. Sometimes the same team, or even the same person, would be responsible for both, but the roles would be separate. The operations people would be in charge of manually figuring out how to hook all the servers together.

Now an app lifecycle management tool can do all that for you. It knows about the application, it knows how to execute the code, it knows how to add the servers and instances to the application. But the app lifecycle management tool itself needs operations. People are required to operate the tool. The difference is that it is an abstract tool into which you can put anything, any application. As a developer, it does not matter if the operations people running the tool are in-house and sitting right next to you, or if they are hundreds of miles away in a place like Portland, Oregon.

Thus we enter the realm of NoOps and Platform-as-a-Service.

The Next-Generation Cloud with Platform-as-a-Service

The cloud has been instrumental in moving us away from a paradigm that involved significant expenses, not only in terms of buying servers, but also of running those systems, with all the personnel involved.

In the past, any startup would have had a similar experience. You would need to hire people to handle your core competency, and then spend millions of dollars to handle all of the data center and management pieces.

The central concept and the main benefit of the cloud, beginning with Infrastructure-as-a-Service, is to reduce the cost of buying data centers. You do not need to buy data centers anymore. But you still need operations people to run the servers that you are now renting.

NoOps fully removes the need for operations and development people to work hand in hand. Operational needs are still being fulfilled, but they are being accomplished independently of any individual application. NoOps refers to the idea of outsourcing operations roles and providing a way for developers to get their jobs done faster. Developers don't have to wait for another team to deploy their code, and the systems that automate those processes for developers operate seamlessly.

NoOps is a controversial term, because some people read it as "No Ops," suggesting that operations are no longer relevant. On the contrary, however, operations are more relevant and important today than ever. The intent behind the term NoOps is to highlight that from the developer's perspective, you no longer interact as directly with the operating guts of running the application. It's the same as how "NoSQL" doesn't mean that SQL is no longer relevant, but rather that there is another way of approaching data storage and retrieval where a developer doesn't interact with SQL.

Platform-as-a-Service outsources operations. It is not getting rid of operations, but decoupling them from development, so that you can get your job as a developer done easier and faster.

The original iterations of managed Platform-as-a-Service, which included systems such as Force.com (*http://force.com*) and the Google App Engine, were very constrained. They required you to develop your code against their APIs, so that they only worked within their contexts. Their Platform-as-a-Service features were accessed only when you tied them directly to their systems. They promised that you could access special data and that you could take advantage of features like auto-scaling—but doing so could be difficult.

There were two downsides to early PaaS. The first was that you needed to learn a new set of APIs in order to program against them, so there was a learning curve just to get acclimated. The second downside involved portability. If you were to program against the Google App Engine, for example, it would be difficult to move your application and try it out on a different platform. There were upsides as well, though such as the extractive system data and the services that they provided.

Then new players began to arrive on the scene, and with their arrival came a movement toward platforms like Heroku and EngineYard. They broke the mold of saying that you needed to code against APIs. They said, in effect, "We are going to take your application as is. You don't have to make any changes that work against proprietary APIs. You can run this code just as easily on your own hardware as you could on our systems, and you aren't going to have to change your code to make that happen." For developers, this was a revolutionary moment in the history of the cloud.

Initially, in order to provide their innovative services, these PaaS providers limited the language technology. Early users of Heroku and EngineYard, for example, could only pick Ruby. So while the upside was that you didn't have to program against APIs, the downside was a restriction on what languages you could pick.

PaaS quickly evolved with the help of next-generation PaaS companies like AppFog and dotCloud, which were no longer tied to a single language. Today, many larger PaaS companies, and even older ones like Heroku and EngineYard, support many programming languages. This represents a significant transition from restrictive platforms to those that are more open.

Some PaaS companies are still tied to single programming languages, however, claiming that there is more benefit in having deeper domain knowledge for a single language.

A popular trend in PaaS with companies like AppFog is multi-infrastructure PaaS. This allows you to run apps in many different infrastructures at the same time, even operated by completely different companies. For the first time in history, you can easily run your app on Amazon Web Services and Rackspace at the same time. If Amazon Web Services goes down, Rackspace can act as a disaster recovery program that keeps applications up and running on a separate system. This has been a dream for most programmers that PaaS can uniquely fulfill.

The Core of the Cloud

For developers, "the cloud" can be a loaded term with many different interpretations. How does the cloud help the developer get her job done better and faster? It can be difficult to clearly determine what is simply an application and what will actually change your life.

To some people, the cloud means Gmail, Dropbox, and similar services. But these are applications *built on* the cloud. They do not change a developer's life. What really changes a developer's life are the core fundamental cloud technologies, the essential technologies that form the backbone of the cloud.

The foundational cloud technologies are virtualization, infrastructure APIs, DevOps, app lifecycle management tools, and NoOps. They all build on top of each other and combine to enable the next generation of technologies. Each one is necessary for the others. For example, you can't have infrastructure APIs for virtualization without virtualization itself.

As a developer, you can interact with any one of these foundational technologies and extract great benefits. For example, you can interact with virtualization directly. Many DevOps technologies do so, managing KVM or Xen directly, usually to virtualize different operating systems and test applications in those systems. You can test an application to determine whether it is a software app, a web app, or a mobile app; with this foundational technology, you can virtualize all of these environments.

Using APIs for virtualization, many developers build on Amazon Web Services and similar OpenStack APIs in order to get their jobs done better and faster. It enables them to spawn servers and manage processes and packages with great speed.

But the problem is that you, Mr. or Ms. Developer, are still the one on call when the servers go down at 4 a.m. And the servers inevitably do go down at 4 a.m. Even with virtualization. Even with infrastructure APIs. Even with Amazon Web Services. Even with Cloud Foundry.

As a developer, half of the problem is getting the resources you need; that is what Infrastructure-as-a-Service solves. The other half of the problem is running and managing your application; that is what Platform-as-a-Service solves.

From a developer's point of view, you can utilize any of these core technologies successfully. The higher up the stack you move, the more time you can spend writing your own code. As a developer, you can spend time at the IaaS level: you'll have more control over some of the lower features, those closer to the infrastructure. The trade-off is that you'll need to spend more time in VMs and less time on the code that you are writing for your users.

The higher up the stack you move in the cloud and the closer you get to PaaS, the more time you can spend innovating. You'll have the time to be like Jason Gendron and improve your product, to pivot and try different things with your users, to figure out how to build the next Google or Facebook, rather than worrying how to keep the servers up at 4 a.m.

Managed Platforms versus Productized Platforms

Our discussion of PaaS has centered on managed or "public cloud" PaaS, in which a developer or company outsources maintenance responsibilities to the PaaS provider. A productized or "private cloud" PaaS offers a different set of attributes.

In a productized platform, you are utilizing app lifecycle management tools and Platform-as-a-Service tools on your own hardware with your own resources. The benefit is that your operations team is in control. They can incorporate the platform's tools in a way that works with many of your applications because they are familiar with how they work. Another advantage: your operations people can reuse much of the hardware in which you have invested and determine how to get all aspects of your system to work together well.

A managed PaaS provider, like Heroku or AppEngine, is in charge of running and maintaining operations for you. As we saw earlier, one of the biggest benefits of Platform-as-a-Service is that it provides the ability to decouple development from operations. Once development is decoupled, the operations do not need to be in house anymore. And if they do not need to be in house, you have to ask yourself, "Is it cheaper to run them in house or is there an economy of scale to be had with an outside provider?"

A managed platform takes PaaS technology and provides it as a service for your company in real time without you needing to worry about service level agreements. Uptime is guaranteed, so that when things go wrong at 4 a.m., it is the public provider's job to fix it, not yours.

There are various productized platforms to choose from. There are open source app lifecycle management tools like Cloud Foundry or OpenShift that can be run on-premises, and there are more commercial tools like Cloudify and Stackato that can be licensed. Some companies, like AppFog, have both a public cloud PaaS offering and a private cloud, on-premises license of the same software.

Running app lifecycle management tools like Cloud Foundry on your own can be very hard. Production-quality service for these tools requires dozens of individual components that interact with each other. It can be a complex matter making sure that these components interact well, that they are healthy and managed, and that if something goes wrong, they are replaced. Those are the kind of issues handled by a managed platform—issues that will need to be dealt with manually if you are trying to incorporate those tools into your own processes.

The Cloud's Promise (or Hype)

From a developer's point of view, part of the challenge of thriving in this new landscape is determining whether or not the cloud is all hype.

Is Gmail going to make a dramatic difference in the life of an individual developer, a corporation, or an agency? Probably not. It might make an incremental improvement, but not a drastic one. However, understanding how to best utilize foundational cloud tools like DevOps and PaaS within the operation of a modern business, whether you are starting one or running one, and figuring out how to leverage cloud technology to do your job faster and more cheaply than before is not hype at all. On the contrary, it is how high-tech companies are going to be built and operated in the future. It is reality. Without a doubt, we are rapidly headed *en masse* to the cloud.

When technology is built on technology, it creates a feedback loop that grows exponentially. When you consider, for example, that the maturing process that led from Morse code to the advent of the telephone took more than 40 years, the current rate of technological maturation is nothing short of astounding. That's one of the lessons of Moore's law on transistors, which observes that the number of transistors on integrated circuits doubles approximately every two years. In high-tech companies and in the cloud, innovations are happening more rapidly than ever. The timeline for new foundational technologies being built, coming to market, and maturing is shortening quickly, with major overhauls on entire industries happening in timelines as short as a few years. In recent history, it took around a decade for virtualization to gain widespread adoption. IaaS has matured nearly as much in only five years. PaaS is likely to be adopted widely in a mere one to two years.

As a developer, learning to adroitly adapt to these technologies is key for growing your career in this modern age.

The Cloud in Five Years

PaaS is maturing quickly, but it is still not perfect for every application. Will the next Twitter or the next Facebook be built on PaaS? The answer today is "not yet," but most companies are at least starting to consider the advantages of moving to PaaS.

As of 2013, PaaS has not been proven at scale yet, much like Ruby on Rails hadn't been in 2006. A few large companies have shown success with PaaS (e.g., Groupon using EngineYard). Once a few more large success stories have shown the potential of PaaS at large scale, we are likely to see a mass adoption shortly after.

The other factor for mass adoption is the maturity of PaaS behind the firewalls for large corporations. Heroku and EngineYard are fantastic public cloud solutions, but large companies have already invested in large numbers of servers that are not likely to be retired very soon. Being able to run large applications in PaaS on existing hardware will go a long way to making mass adoption a reality.

If you look ahead 5 to 10 years, PaaS will be a cornerstone technology. We are going to witness a new generation of high-tech companies being built on the tools of the cloud. We are going to see billion-dollar companies being built solely on PaaS technology.

The Promise Fulfilled

As we saw at the beginning of this chapter, PaaS literally changed Jason Gendron's life situation. It enabled him to focus on his core talents, writing code and running his business, while it lowered his cost of innovation. It gave him the time and the server power to help turn TwitClub into a successful venture.

By removing the need for an IaaS provider, by managing the nitty gritty of day-to-day operations, by handling glitches and crashes, PaaS is changing the lives of millions of other developers.

Whether you are inside an agency dealing with hundreds of clients, inside an enterprise with thousands of users, or working on your own to develop the big idea, PaaS offers you the tools to realize your potential.

It reduces the price of innovation for individual developers. It reduces the price of innovation for venture capitalists looking to invest in the next Google. And it is going to bring the same cost savings into enterprises as enterprise adoption of PaaS becomes ubiquitous.

In the coming chapters, we'll look more closely at PaaS and managed services, examine how to write apps for PaaS, and explore a future in which PaaS becomes a major player in cloud technology.

CHAPTER 2

What Is PaaS?

Developers are migrating to PaaS to get their jobs done faster and better.

Faster: because you spend less time setting up and managing servers, or waiting for someone else to do it.

Better: because PaaS lets you implement best practices without thinking about it.

Developers all have their own unique sets of considerations and challenges. Before writing this book, I myself had challenges rooted in a childhood web success that turned into what would have been a crushing failure had I not learned some critical lessons that strongly influence how I write code today.

Conjuring a Website

In 1996, my family signed up for an Internet connection and received a shared hosting account tied to our Internet Service Provider. I downloaded Fetch, a free FTP client, and found a Webmonkey tutorial that taught me the basics of HTML. I entered my FTP credentials and was on my way. When I fully realized anyone in the world could see my Hello World web app, I was hooked. A simple "hello" transformed the rest of my life.

I love magic. I find it fascinating how you can prepare for days or even weeks, practicing detailed finger work for a trick that can last a few seconds. I wanted to combine my passion for doing magic tricks with my passion for this new toy called the Web. So I created my first web page, a page for magicians to exchange ideas and tricks. It started out as a simple HTML page and quickly grew into a dynamic PHP website that I called The Conjuring Cabaret.

As the community grew, The Conjuring Cabaret became more and more dynamic, adding content, functionality, and design. Many magicians contributed magic tricks and tips. There were tests that visitors had to pass in order to get in to see those tricks, making sure that only real magicians could access this inner sanctum.

The site grew to the point that it needed its own server. The Conjuring Cabaret was hosted on a dedicated box, and I was thrilled. By 2001, it was among the top magic websites, with hundreds of tricks and thousands of members. I was installing and configuring Apache and MySQL and spent countless nights tuning things to be just right.

Then one day I woke up and the website was not working. I tried to log into the server. No luck. I tried to email the managed server provider and didn't hear back. I kept emailing them, and a few days later, when they finally replied, they said, "Sorry, your server died."

I said, "What do you mean my server died?"

Like many developers before and since, I had never gotten around to backing up my server. I lost all of the data, all of the magic tricks, and all of the users. Ironically, that server had performed a magic trick of the highest order: it made everything disappear.

That was the end of my first website.

It was a painful episode and a pivotal moment for me, deeply influencing my professional life. Years later, I was able to realize a dream that came out of that pain when I began to use Platform-as-a-Service and founded a PaaS provider called AppFog.

Early Options for Developers

Episodes of scaling problems and losing data are unfortunately common, mainly because application developers have had only a few options in the last generation. Chief among them were shared web hosting and dedicated web hosting. Now we can add into the mix a powerful, relatively new alternative called Platform-as-a-Service. Before we look more deeply at PaaS, let's examine the first two options.

Shared Web Hosting

Traditionally, shared web hosting has been the easiest way for web developers to get started. Examples include GoDaddy, Yahoo!, Comcast, and many ISPs to this day.

The central concept revolves around an FTP account. You get credentials for your FTP application server. That server hosts thousands, sometimes tens of thousands, of websites. Usually the server is large, but it can very quickly get bogged down. If one or two of those websites start to get popular, even with a powerful server, it might be enough to soak up all of the resources. The result: tens of thousands of websites could become very slow or might not even respond.

The upside to shared hosting is price. Shared hosting is cheap, sometimes even free. Also, it's a hands-free account. You don't have to do security patches. You don't have to manage the software. You don't have to know anything about how the software is written. All you need to know is how to write some HTML code; you hand it over, and everything else is handled for you. But because it's so inexpensive, your provider can't afford to handle things well at all times. It can't scale. It can't go beyond its capabilities, but it usually does work for simple situations.

While it's an economy of scale for the hosting provider, it's not a reliable system for putting up a storefront, a complicated website, or even a site that you want your clients to be able to reliably visit to get your contact information.

Another pitfall of shared hosting is security. Your code can be on the same system as over 10,000 other pieces of code. Keep in mind that a normal website can easily get hundreds of security attacks every day. Multiply that by tens of thousands of pieces of code that aren't yours, and you can see the risks involved in running a production site on a shared system.

Despite its disadvantages, developers still find shared web hosting useful to host personal web pages, to put up simple ideas, and to try out new ideas. It's useful for development when you're not sure if you want to invest the kind of money it would take to run your own servers, and when you don't need to scale yet. The trouble is that when you do need to scale, it can become a painful process to move from a shared to a dedicated system.

Dedicated Hosting

Developers, especially web developers, have traditionally used shared web hosting to get started because it's cheap and easy. When they look to graduate beyond that, they often turn to dedicated web hosting. This could be as simple as hosting your own server at home using your Internet connection. But there are several other options that provide varying degrees of service and scalability.

Here is a generalized list of dedicated hosting options, sorted by decreasing order of control (and typically, performance):

- Colocated servers
- Managed servers
- Virtual private servers
- Infrastructure-as-a-Service

Let's now take a look at each of these in more depth.

Colocated servers

With colocation, you usually buy your servers yourself. Then you ship them to a high-bandwidth data center where you pay a monthly fee. The colocation facility gives you Internet access and sometimes will even help debug or restart a server. But in addition to the up-front costs of the machines, you are responsible for maintaining and managing the servers.

Managed servers

The term "managed server" is a bit of a misnomer. In reality, the management of the server can be quite limited. If the RAM becomes corrupt, they will replace it for you. If there are hardware issues, the provider will replace your hardware. But while they replace disks or RAM, they do not replace your data, so it's critical to make sure that you have off-site backups.

There are various benefits to using managed servers. Often you do not have to buy the servers yourself; you lease them from the same provider that is hosting and managing them. They are faster than some of the other dedicated alternatives, as well as more reliable and more robust. Managed servers can and do die, but they usually don't die very quickly. You generally have to wait for a disk failure, which on average could take a year or two. Compare that to the ephemeral servers on Amazon Web Services, which could die in a matter of days or weeks. The downside is that provisioning new servers can easily take anywhere from weeks to a month.

Virtual private servers

Virtual private servers, or VPS, are similar to managed servers, but virtualized. In desktop environments, you may be familiar with Parallels, VirtualBox, and Fusion. For server-side virtualization, the tools of the trade (known as *hypervisors*) include Xen-Server, KVM, Virtuozzo, Vserver, and Hyper-V.

Virtualization allows large servers with many terabytes of RAM and hundreds of processor cores to be subdivided into smaller virtual servers with gigabytes of RAM and one to four cores. This makes these servers a lot easier to start, run, and replace than non-virtualized dedicated servers.

Virtualization technology allows for each virtual machine to act independently of one another in terms of security, isolating processes and tenants in a much more comprehensive way than sharing servers through multitenant shared hosts all on a single Apache instance. Each virtual machine has its own root account and, if compromised, does not have access to any other of the virtual machines.

The downside to VPS can be that since the underlying physical resources can be shared, you can still run into issues where a neighboring tenant is hogging your CPU or disk I/O, which can slow down your applications unless you plan for these kinds of inconsistencies.

Infrastructure-as-a-Service

IaaS is like an on-demand elastic VPS with an API. It is the fastest version of dedicated web hosting in the sense of provisioning. But it is still considered to be dedicated web hosting because you still get root access. The largest effective difference from other kinds of hosting is that you can go from requesting new servers to having them up and running in about 30 seconds. They can be dedicated real servers, but usually are virtual servers. Virtualization is accomplished with software that ranges from VMware's vSphere to Xen from Citrix all the way to Microsoft Hyper-V. The most popular Infrastructure-as-a-Service is Amazon Web Services, which uses Xen to virtualize its hardware.

With IaaS, what you get are dedicated servers with dedicated IP addresses. They start out as a blank slate, so you have to do all the system administration: install the software, install Apache, configure Apache, secure the server, tune the server, tune Apache, tune MySQL, add the accounts, distribute passwords, set up SSH, put the SSH keys in, install the packages, upgrade the packages, and make sure your app works with the versions of software included on the machine.

The benefits of IaaS are the ability to provision as many servers as you need and the ability to do so very quickly on demand. The downside is that those servers are generally slower than their dedicated alternatives. They also offer less performance and they are less reliable, so they tend to be ephemeral, meaning that they go down without notice. You have to design your system to be able to handle servers dying at will, adding a layer of complication.

Comparing costs

The cost structures for the various forms of dedicated web hosting are vastly different.

In the colocated version, you have the initial fixed costs associated with buying the machines. You're only renting space in the colocation facility, though, so the ongoing costs are significantly lower compared to similar IaaS usage. Many large applications go the colocation route, investing in their own hardware to take advantage of the monthly cost savings. This is also known as increasing capital expense (capex) in order to reduce daily operating expense (opex). Colocation costs vary but can start at around $1,000 per month for a rack, which can hold up to 16 servers. Keep in mind, however, that you're still in charge of maintaining and managing the machines. You will need to go in, install the machines, wire them together, and maintain them in person as they fail.

On the other end of the spectrum is Infrastructure-as-a-Service. With IaaS, you pay an hourly cost based only on the resources you need (also known as increasing opex to reduce up-front capex). Generally there are a wide variety of different combinations from which to pick, including different CPU speeds, disk sizes, and I/O performance.

Since IaaS is typically priced by the hour and has no long-term commitment, it's very handy for cases in which you need to provision many servers and use them for a short amount of time—performing a vast calculation over a specified amount of data, for example. How would such a scenario impact your budget?

Let's suppose you're going to sequence DNA. You have a set problem and you have a set piece of data. Using Infrastructure-as-a-Service, you can spin up a thousand servers, sequence the DNA over a set period of time, and then shut the servers down. You only pay for the hours that the servers were running. Instead of buying a thousand servers that sit around doing nothing after you've finished sequencing the DNA, you set up only what you need for the time you need it.

Web applications tend to live much longer than a DNA sequencing can take, which might on the surface seem to favor capex over opex, because you can make long-term commitments. This can make IaaS seem economically unfavorable for hosting web applications. However, web applications might experience spikes. If you're preparing to go on a talk show or a news program, you need to be prepared to handle the resulting traffic to your website. With a colocated facility, you would have to order the servers, wait a few weeks, then bring them in and have them configured, which could take another few weeks. With Infrastructure-as-a-Service, you can make an automated API call 24 hours a day and add a thousand servers to your system that can be available within minutes. After the traffic diminishes, you can deprovision the servers and only have to pay for the time that you used.

The general problem with Infrastructure-as-a-Service is that since the servers are ephemeral, you need to have some kind of persistent block storage so that you can keep your data. For example, if you have a MySQL database and the server goes down, you don't want to lose that data. You must have the data persisted on block storage or some other similar persistent storage technology. These and other services add additional hourly charges.

Infrastructure-as-a-Service is an *à la carte* system. You can add services as you need to and then pay for them on an hourly basis.

PaaS: The Best of Both Worlds

As a developer, the general tendency is to start out with shared hosting. Soon you might experience a need to have more power and control, so you move into dedicated hosting. You feel a rush because you now have ultimate control. You're excited to be tuning your servers and learning how to make them run faster. You're excited because your website loads faster and it can handle more users.

However, the excitement quickly dissipates as time goes on, because the overhead of taking care of those servers day after day wears you down. You want the power and control that come with dedicated servers, but before too long your servers get hacked into and you are fully responsible for fixing them. Then the database gets corrupted, and you have to restore your backups on your own.

But wait, there's more! It's not only the time and effort of managing your machines. When the server dies at 4 a.m. (and it always does so at the most inconvenient times), you are always ultimately responsible for fixing it. If you're at dinner, you have to go. If you're at a wedding, you have to go. If you're on vacation, you have to go. This is why pagers exist—for doctors and system administrators.

In short, from a developer's point of view, shared web hosting is easy but does not provide enough control and power, and dedicated hosting is powerful but provides too many distractions and too much overhead. Until the advent of Platform-as-a-Service, there was never an in-between.

Combine the power of dedicated hosting together with the ease of shared hosting and you get Platform-as-a-Service.

The Developer's Holy Grail

Let's return briefly to the example in which you've made a TV appearance and your website suddenly experiences a spike in traffic. The problem with dedicated hosting is moving from a single server to 100 servers. It's a potential nightmare because you'll need to hire a team of people to help manage those 100 servers. With Platform-as-a-Service, moving from a single server behind your app to 100 servers can take seconds. All you do is move a slider from the left to the right.

As you'll see, Platform-as-a-Service can provide the power, speed, reliability, and scalability that you wanted with dedicated hosting, and yet be as simple to use as shared hosting. You might go so far as to say that Platform-as-a-Service is the developer's Holy Grail of scalability and reliability.

This enhanced reliability comes courtesy of one of the key tenets of scalable architecture in the modern web development era: *N-tier architecture.*

Sharing the Load

With N-tier application architecture, you don't put your app logic on the same servers as your database servers or caching servers or load balancers. You have different layers of servers that handle different aspects of the application independently.

You do this for horizontal scalability, so that you can add more capacity by simply adding more of a certain kind of service in parallel and then configuring the software to distribute the load. So now you have gone from having a single server to at least three or four layers of servers, or *tiers*. Within each of those tiers, you're replicating for failover and high availability.

This architecture is what you usually end up piecing together when you are using dedicated servers. But every Platform-as-a-Service has N-tier built into it from the start. It's packaged into the offerings as a de facto standard from the ground up, blending a best-of-breed approach to dedicated web hosting with a simple deployment strategy for deploying your code.

Language Considerations

There are a number of different approaches to Platform-as-a-Service. Some vendors focus on a single programming language, meaning you'll be restricted to working only with Java, or PHP, or Python, or Node.js.

Other PaaS vendors let you choose from a variety of different languages. On the one hand, a multilanguage provider has the benefit of being a one-stop shop. On the other hand, you will sometimes have a more highly tuned environment with a single-language PaaS provider. In general, the most widely used PaaS systems tend to be multilanguage.

One should also be aware of vendor lock-in issues. Some Platform-as-a-Service providers require you to program against their APIs, and once you have tied your code to their APIs it can be very difficult to move it anywhere else. If this is simply at the level of database services, your code can still remain quite portable. However, if there are custom libraries and custom code APIs, it can be problematic and sometimes impossible to compartmentalize these integration points to the point that you can quickly move your app to another PaaS provider.

PaaS Pricing

Almost every Platform-as-a-Service provider lets you try it for free. Usually you can set up at least a few applications for free. This is a useful way for developers to get started and familiarize themselves with Platform-as-a-Service. Once you want to deploy a production application, there are many options, with pricing models that vary depending on which platform you choose. Rates for production-ready apps in PaaS can run from as little as $20 per month to thousands of dollars per month.

For example, with one leading PaaS service you can deploy applications for free, but when you want to scale those applications and add more instances behind them (making them production-ready), you start paying on a per-instance basis. Those instances can each cost $30–40 a month. If you want background processing, that is another $30–40 a month. So, with some Platform-as-a-Service providers, the price can grow quickly as your application needs to scale.

Other platforms have different pricing models. Some charge based on how many virtual machines you use. Others charge on a resource consumption model. With AppFog, you have a set amount of RAM; within that amount of RAM you can deploy as many applications, or as many instances behind those applications, as you want. The monthly fee is based on how much RAM you need, not how you use it. dotCloud has a similar model.

Is PaaS Really New or Just IaaS++?

Several questions arise. Is Platform-as-a-Service a new concept? Or is it simply an extension of Infrastructure-as-a-Service? Is the "big idea" the concept of APIs with provisioning servers? Or is Platform-as-a-Service a new and separate kind of idea?

There is a strong case to be made that IaaS and PaaS are very different from one another and that Platform-as-a-Service is not a feature of Infrastructure-as-a-Service. Fundamentally, it comes down to what is important to each service.

What are the central concepts behind IaaS and PaaS? Another way to ask this question is this: what are their atomic units?

Looking at atomic units

An atomic unit is the least divisible unit of interest for an entity. What is the least common factor? What is the base indivisible aspect that people care about? In math, it's numbers (or even more fundamentally, sets). In physics, it's equations. In chemistry, it's molecules. In biology, it's cells.

This applies in the business world, as well. For McDonald's, it's hamburgers. For Barnes & Noble, it's books. For Coca-Cola, it's a can of Coke. It is the base unit that the company cares most about.

Figuring out the atomic unit for a company is both enlightening and limiting. Enlightening because it gives you a focus—it lets you rally to what you are good at—and limiting because it is incredibly difficult to be as good at selling anything outside the purview of your atomic units. Few companies who try to have multiple atomic units are able to succeed.

The atomic unit does not have to be as specific as the examples just given. For Amazon.com, it's anything you can warehouse and ship in a box. For Netflix, it's digital media in various forms. For Procter & Gamble, it's household items.

When it comes to sorting out atomic units, there is a major amount of confusion in the cloud. Part of the reason for this confusion is that many different companies who sell many different atomic units are being grouped together. One way to make sense of it all is by understanding the atomic units of these companies at a generic level.

IaaS versus PaaS

For Infrastructure-as-a-Service, the atomic unit is resources. By resources, we mean servers, disks, networks, and IP addresses. IaaS is all about providing these resources on demand. For example, when you look at Amazon Web Services, all the tools center around resources, all the documentation is about resources, all development is focused on resources, and the main thing people use it for is resources. Other IaaS examples include Rackspace, GoGrid, and Joyent.

For Platform-as-a-Service, the atomic unit is applications. What is an application? It's a system. It's a combination of code and all the services that communicate with that code at any point in time. It is not a resource. In fact, an app is composed of many individual resources all tied together. The amount of effort required to connect those resources together is often underestimated. That's why companies hire IT departments and why system administrators are always in demand. Going from a single host running Apache and MySQL all in one to a system architecture with separate load balancers, caching servers, app servers, and database servers with redundancy and failover involves a lot of work, both up front and later on in maintenance.

The other thing that PaaS does is configure and manage IaaS from an apps perspective. Tools like Cloud Formation are great, but they approach IaaS management from a resources perspective. Apps see the world in a much different way than resources do.

Apps, unlike resources, do not tend to come and go frequently. The need for on-demand hourly pricing, while highly useful for IaaS, is not as important with this model, except when you temporarily burst app usage or you're in a test/dev scenario.

In short, Platform-as-a-Service providers deal with code and services. The responsibility of those providers is to manage and maintain the code, to run the services, and to make certain that the connections between everything remain up and running at all times.

PaaS: A Vital Tool for Modern Apps

Application development has drastically changed in the last generation. From the early days of code running on computers the size of buildings to client/server architectures and now modern REST APIs, the tools used to build and run code have changed as well.

Moving Toward Higher-Level Languages

Let's return to an earlier example: when you want to sequence DNA, you want to do it as quickly as possible, so you use low-level languages like C and Assembly to get as much performance as you can.

In PaaS, the tendency is more toward building out web applications, and latency is not as critically important. The quality that is valued more highly for the types of applications that run on PaaS is the ability to create things quickly and connect them quickly. The higher-level languages—the dynamic scripting languages like Ruby, PHP, Python, and Node.js—are better suited to this than some of the lower-level languages.

Thus, the tendency within PaaS is toward languages that a few decades ago were thought of merely as scripting languages. Now they have become powerful tools for businesses to power their applications. Facebook, one of the biggest sites on the Internet, uses PHP to power its systems. Yahoo! also used PHP. Twitter was initially built on Ruby. LinkedIn used Ruby, then changed to Node.js. So you can see a proliferation of web content being built on dynamic languages.

Managing the Backend

The new generation of languages is also breeding a new style of development: quick iterations on smaller sections of code, faster production of applications that are smaller and at scale. The applications that are generally being built are API-type applications. Examples of these kinds of applications (on a larger scale) include Gmail, Twitter, and MobileMe, which use APIs to communicate with their web frontends. Those same APIs can be used in the context of mobile applications, making sure that a mobile app can register users and that users can communicate with each other. This all must happen through APIs and backend services.

Managing the backend for a mobile application can easily take more time than building it in the first place, which is why Platform-as-a-Service is such a vital tool. If you have a mobile app that gets on the Apple App Store's top 10 list, you need to make sure that your backend application can scale with the needs of your user growth and can handle millions of users accessing it from their phones every minute. Traditionally, this has taken armies of IT and ops people. Platform-as-a-Service gives you the ability to manage hundreds or even thousands of backends simply with a slider, rather than with a team of people.

In case this remains unclear, it should be stated that PaaS puts control and power into the hands of the developer. At long last, that pager has been rendered unnecessary. PaaS won't eliminate code bugs, obviously, but hardware and infrastructure failure should not be concerns for developers anymore.

Conjuring Confidence

Years after I lost my own website, Platform-as-a-Service emerged. With PaaS emerged the opportunity to get apps up and running faster and more easily than ever before. Now backing up applications can happen with a click of a button. You don't have to worry about servers going down because there are people out there worrying for you. PaaS renews confidence and vigor for all of the applications that modern developers deploy.

The days of dreaded phone calls where people tell you that your servers have died will become history as you adopt PaaS and utilize it to its full potential.

CHAPTER 3

Types of PaaS

In the previous chapters we briefly discussed the concept of portability, which lets you move applications and deploy them on different systems. While portability is in many cases an attractive feature, there are trade-offs to both portable and non-portable PaaS.

Non-Portable: Following a Template

With a non-portable PaaS you build an application by writing code around the unique specifications and APIs of that platform.

This means that the structure of your code needs to adhere very strictly to a certain template or API. The APIs might be centered on the service's databases, storage mechanisms, or search mechanisms. Other times, the APIs are lower level and code related. Sometimes you must even use specialized languages that are built only for that platform.

As you can see, there can be various types of hooks into a platform that make it non-portable. The earliest forms of Platform-as-a-Service were built around these highly structured ideas. They were the underpinnings of the early experiments that turned into what we now know as Platform-as-a-Service.

But questions quickly arose. Why should you write your code around a proprietary API? Are the benefits and access to the data worth the lack of flexibility? Before we examine how a new generation of companies answered those questions, let's take a look at some of the major players in the non-portable PaaS category.

Force.com

Launched in 2008, Force.com (*http://force.com*), Salesforce's developer platform, allows you to build applications that extend the functionality of Salesforce (*http://www.sales force.com/*), a very popular SaaS customer relationship management (CRM) sales tool. This was one of the first incarnations of PaaS as we know it today. Force.com inspired a generation of applications, and thousands of developers built new ways to access and analyze Salesforce's rich dataset.

The Force.com Platform-as-a-Service provides Web Service APIs and toolkits, a user interface for building apps, a database for persistent data, and basic website hosting functionality. More recently, it has added mobile capabilities that make it easy to create mobile applications using the Force.com PaaS as well.

The downside to using Force.com is that you cannot build general-purpose applications using any programming language you want. Application logic is built and run using Apex, a strongly typed, object-oriented, Java-like language that runs on Force.com. The upside is that getting started creating new applications is simple and fast using the web-based interface. You choose the data types you want to collect, creating data structures that can autogenerate web and mobile interfaces for collecting that data.

On top of data input options, you can also add formulas, approval processes, email sending, and tests very quickly and easily. The Force.com PaaS even has its own Force.com IDE for developing, testing, and deploying applications quickly and easily.

When you work within the constraints of the Force.com platform, you do not have to worry about scaling or managing your application; Salesforce does that for you. This idea is the foundation from which PaaS has gained popularity.

As the Force.com platform has matured, more and more services have been added: one example is Database.com (*http://database.com*), a database service with custom APIs and data feeds for building applications used by around 100,000 businesses worldwide.

Google App Engine

Google App Engine (*https://developers.google.com/appengine/*) (GAE), also launched in 2008, was one of the very earliest forms of PaaS. Its promise was that you could tap into the vast power of Google, draw on Google's computing resources, and use Google's infrastructure and expertise in running and operating machines. The caveat was that your application would have to adhere to Google's standards. Google has built not only an operations team, but also a set of tools and systems that work in a specific way—and they work that way in order to scale to "Google scale."

What kind of scale are we talking about? A very large one in which you are dealing with many, many thousands of machines all working together to solve a single problem. When you are dealing with a scale as large as Google's, the tools are very prescriptive; they need to be in order to process volumes of data that are so immense. Google literally processes the entire Internet. One of the central ideas of GAE is that if you adhere to its standards, you too could have that power inside your application, and only pay for the processing power that you use.

Here it becomes evident why GAE is non-portable. It has an existing infrastructure that you are allowed to tap into only if you play by Google's set of rules. On the one hand, you have to write your code around Google's expectations. On the other hand, if you do so, you gain the benefits of being able to run at Google scale.

Many PaaS platforms have limitations of various types. When you are dealing with a non-portable PaaS such as GAE, those limitations can be strict. You have to adhere very closely to them in order to take advantage of GAE's features.

With GAE, there are limitations on access to the filesystem, on access to memory, on the amount of memory you can tap into, and on how long your processes can run.

These limitations can force a developer to think in different ways. For example, let's suppose you have a website that needs to compile a large list of information and compute data for each item on that list. In a traditional hosting environment, when a user makes a request to such a site, delivering results can take a significant amount of time. All of the processing must happen before the response goes back to the user. And, depending on the complexity of this processing, it could easily take seconds.

This is where we encounter another of the limitations within GAE: there is a set amount of time within which your application must respond. If it doesn't respond fast enough, GAE will kill the process.

But this can actually be a positive factor in the development of the user experience if the application is designed to know that it cannot live that long. It forces the developer to ask himself, "Instead of simply doing it the way I always have done it, how does Google want me to do it?" So, instead of compiling the list every time a user hits the website, you could create a cache and serve up the list from the cache. The cache could serve very quickly and provide a better user experience. In order to compile that cache in the background, you would have to use a different set of Google tools to do those calculations in a more scalable fashion, and then put those into the caching database.

GAE has a large following and a large developer mindshare behind it. Its promise—taking advantage of the power of Google—has helped make it a leader in the non-portable PaaS category.

Windows Azure

Microsoft also thought very hard about how to build a Platform-as-a-Service. Its expertise with the .NET Framework led the company to consider the best way to accomplish this around .NET. In 2008, Microsoft launched Windows Azure (*http://www.windowsazure.com/*).

The company set out to create a set of libraries. These were designed in such a way that if a developer were to incorporate them into her system, Azure would take advantage of those libraries in order to scale the system. Microsoft also provides standard services that can scale independently.

With Windows Azure, you have basic systems, like a message bus and queuing systems, and a variety of different options based on the specific needs of your application. These provide patterns for developers to build distributed applications that can interact with each other over networks. If you incorporate through the libraries the technologies and services that Microsoft has built, you can take advantage of the Azure system and be able to scale your application fairly quickly and easily.

Recently, Microsoft has taken steps to move away from a non-portable Azure system, decoupling some of the requirements that tie developers into required services. This has allowed expansion into different languages and technologies, taking Azure from a non-portable PaaS more into the portable realm, which requires no changes to the code in order for it to run. So, Azure is actually a system that started out as non-portable and has been moving slowly toward portability. In fact, Microsoft recently released a very portable version of its Platform-as-a-Service.

Non-Portable Conclusion

Although all of these PaaS options started out as non-portable, many of them are adding functionality that makes them more and more portable every day. GAE has released PHP support that requires fewer and fewer changes to work out of the box. Windows Azure has also released PHP support, and developers can do more without programming against the Microsoft APIs than ever before.

Portable: No Heavy Lifting Required

A portable PaaS is a platform built to run code without requiring significant changes to how that code is written. For developers who have created code to run in shared hosting or dedicated hosting environments, moving that code into a portable Platform-as-a-Service should not be difficult. There are no required service hubs that need to be adhered to in order to run your applications.

There are still limitations, and they can be somewhat challenging to get around, but those limitations are much more functional rather than code related.

Portability broadens the amount and types of code that you can write for Platform-as-a-Service. It also broadens the language support and allows for more flexibility. If you want to move an application between different portable PaaS platforms, you will need to change some aspects of how your application works, but typically those changes will not involve a complete rewrite of your system.

In contrast, look at the early days of Google App Engine, which at the time only supported Python; you needed to write a particular version of Python with certain functions enabled. That limited you: for example, you couldn't run one of the most popular Python frameworks, Django. It's a problem you would never encounter today on a portable Platform-as-a-Service.

Heroku

Heroku (*https://www.heroku.com/*), founded in 2007, was one of the earliest companies offering a portable Platform-as-a-Service. Heroku saw what Force.com and Google App Engine were doing and concluded that forcing developers to write their code against its APIs didn't make as much sense as just letting any code be written.

Heroku started out as a Ruby-only independent startup company, allowing Ruby code to be deployed in any form. It has since been acquired by Salesforce.com and has expanded its language offerings. However, Heroku still doesn't let you write to the filesystem. The rationale is that this makes it easier to create more instances of your app (Heroku calls them "dynos"). If you were to upload or change a piece of code, it would only end up running on a single dyno, and if your application runs on 100 dynos, the uploaded file would not be propagated, leaving an inconsistent dyno. In order to prevent that problem, Heroku simply says that you cannot write to the filesystem (except for an ephemeral temporary directory).

As with Google App Engine, there is also a certain amount of time (although it's more generous with Heroku) that an application can survive for before it is timed out. But there are also tasks that can run in the background and do some work that is asynchronous. These ideas were pioneered by Heroku and set some of the early standards for what can be done with portable Platform-as-a-Service.

A further comparison of Heroku to Google App Engine illustrates some of the key differences between portable and non-portable PaaS.

With Google App Engine, you have to be very strict about the code you are writing, making sure that it adheres specifically to Google's APIs. With Heroku, the code you write—whether it is on a shared or dedicated host—is the same as it is on Heroku. The difference in portability has to do with writing your code against the provider's system versus writing it in a generic way. The reason it becomes portable is that you can take that same code from Heroku and run it on your own systems without having to make major modifications to it.

One of Heroku's other innovations revolves around deploying code. The early PaaS offerings, like Google App Engine, had programs through which you would deploy your code. Heroku took a more general approach and created a git-based deployment system (git is a source-controlled management tool that lets you keep revisions of your software over time, like CVS and other source-control tools).

At Heroku, when you commit your code into the git source control, pushing the code into Heroku triggers a deployment. It's a very quick and easy way to allow developers to deploy their code, unlike trigger shell hosting systems that generally use FTP. With FTP, you have to look for files that have changed and make sure you upload them and sync them. But git will track the file changes over time and keep a history of those changes so you don't have to go hunting for files that have changed. It identifies them and sends those files to the platform automatically.

Cloud Foundry

Built by VMware, Cloud Foundry (*http://www.cloudfoundry.com/*) is a generational new technology that is centered around PaaS. A more recent creation than either Google App Engine or Heroku, it comprises a set of programs and services that let you run your own Platform-as-a-Service. It is open source licensed (Apache 2) and can even be run on your laptop.

With Cloud Foundry, you have access to a set of packages and programs that allow you to interact and deploy code with the same feel as PaaS. It will manage your code and let you scale it up and down in the ways you are used to with a Platform-as-a-Service.

Because it is an open source program, it is significantly different from Heroku, Google App Engine, or Windows Azure. Each of those is a hosted managed service: you do not get to look at the source code, nor do you get to modify those services. Essentially, they are take-it-or-leave-it situations, black boxes into which you enter your code, which is then deployed.

Cloud Foundry has many of the features of PaaS, but it is not a managed service. Like Apache, it's a technology that you have to run yourself. However, it is a complex distributed system and is quite a bit harder to run than a typical system such as Apache.

It is not a system that you can sign up for publicly. If you want to sign up, you have to look for a public provider of Cloud Foundry. Their numbers are growing: AppFog is one, and VMware offers it as a hosted service so you can try it.

In contrast to Heroku, instead of using a git-deploy mechanism, Cloud Foundry created a REST API, a new way to think about deploying code. It uses a Ruby-based command line tool to deploy code. Because it is a REST API, it gives you the flexibility to make your own decisions about whether you want git integration, CVS, Subversion, Darcs, Mercurial, Team Foundation, or anything else. If you want a different kind of version control for your code, it doesn't prescribe one for you and lets you use whichever one you want.

Cloud Foundry also made some other innovative decisions around how to support third-party services. With Heroku and other Platform-as-a-Service technologies, one of the quick benefits is the ability to provision services and have them tie into your application. Traditionally, the way that has happened has been by setting environmental values that are passed along to your application through the runtime. They can be read into the application to get the credentials for your database. Cloud Foundry supports a very similar mechanism, but it has wrapped the idea of services—like MySQL, Postgres, and Redis—into an abstraction that lets you bind services to and unbind them from applications; it keeps an environmental variable array available so that you can iterate through them programmatically.

Cloud Foundry also lets you bind a single data source to multiple applications, which is handy when you need to debug an application and determine its state—either in production data or as an audit system. You can bind your data source simultaneously to various different applications.

One of Heroku's innovations is centered on a third-party add-on marketplace. Via this marketplace, Heroku can provision other cloud tools and, using the environmental variables, pass along the credentials for those tools to your application. Some PaaS platforms, like AppFog, have incorporated a similar idea, but Cloud Foundry does not currently have third-party integration built in.

Service binding is one of the few aspects within a portable Platform-as-a-Service that does actually require a difference in code. When you are trying to move an application from one Platform-as-a-Service to another, generally the part that will result in a difference is how it connects to the database or data sources. Often there are dissimilarities that do require some code—usually a small amount—to be rewritten.

AppFog

CloudFoundry.org (*http://cloudfoundry.org*) pushed the boundaries of Platform-as-a-Service by providing an open source tool set that any developer could use. It also pushed into new territory because it was not a managed Platform-as-a-Service. From the developer's point of view this meant that before you could use Cloud Foundry, you would have to set it up yourself and then run it. If you were going to use it in production, you would have to set it up and run it in production, which, while offering a great amount of flexibility, cuts back on the ease of use typically associated with PaaS.

AppFog (*https://www.appfog.com/*) is a Platform-as-a-Service that is managed and maintained, and it incorporates Cloud Foundry technology. AppFog started as an independent startup and was acquired by CenturyLink in 2013.

One of the other innovations of Heroku is that it was entirely built on Amazon Web Services, and to this day it continues to run on AWS. This is very different from earlier PaaS providers such as Force.com, Google App Engine, and Azure. Each of these was built on top of its own platforms and infrastructures. Cloud Foundry has two components: the open source library called CloudFoundry.org and a proprietary hosted managed platform called CloudFoundry.com, which uses CloudFoundry.org code.

AppFog is a company that also uses CloudFoundry.org code and runs it on multiple infrastructures and public cloud systems. So, while it does run on Amazon Web Services, it is also compatible with OpenStack platforms like Rackspace, HP Cloud, and others. It can even run on private cloud instances of OpenStack and vSphere.

From a developer's point of view, AppFog has many of the features of CloudFoundry.org that you'd find out of the box. But it runs on many infrastructures, letting you choose them and giving you the portability of those infrastructures, as well as the code. Additionally, AppFog has taken the ideas of other platforms, like integration with third-party cloud services, and incorporated those into its platform. The result: you can sign up and run your applications in any cloud infrastructure that you want, using a technology that you can run yourself, giving you the benefits you'll find in other systems (like Heroku) that incorporate third-party add-ons.

dotCloud

There are other platforms that focus specifically on the infrastructure behind the PaaS and spend less time on the user experience. dotCloud (*https://www.dotcloud.com/*) is an example of a Platform-as-a-Service that innovated by being the first to support multiple languages and technologies, and it has popularized the idea of Linux containers with an open source project called Docker (*https://github.com/dotcloud/docker*).

When dotCloud was released, Heroku had been focusing only on Ruby, Google App Engine only on Python, and Azure only on .NET. dotCloud came along and offered support for Python, Java, Ruby, and other technologies.

This popular Platform-as-a-Service has focused on creating a system that works though the command line, similar to Cloud Foundry. It has a Unix command line and an API to interact with that command line, enabling you to deploy your applications in multiple languages.

One of the differences between Cloud Foundry and dotCloud is how they approach language support. With Cloud Foundry, the entire system is an open source tool, which means that you can go in and change the way that applications are run and managed; management is tightly coupled to the Cloud Foundry tool set. dotCloud has abstracted the way that applications are run; you can manage the way they are run within the specifications while you deploy your application.

CloudBees

CloudBees (*http://www.cloudbees.com/*) is a Platform-as-a-Service that is focused specifically on Java. It has been built around Java tool sets and incorporates common tools used within Java platforms.

One aspect that separates CloudBees from other platforms is its integration with continuous integration tools such as Jenkins. In fact, CloudBees has hired some of the people that maintain Jenkins and has become a leader in the continuous integration space. This has given Platform-as-a-Service a new twist because it allows for systems and extends the broader view of PaaS. With other platforms, the idea is to take your code and deploy it into production; CloudBees incorporates more development tools to extend the purview of what it provides.

Instead of simply taking code and putting it into production, CloudBees provides a system that lets you test that code in a continuous manner, making sure that it works before it goes into production. It provides a longer pipeline before your code is deployed and extends some of the functionality for how a developer can work with her Platform-as-a-Service. To date, however, CloudBees still only supports Java and Java-enabled applications. So, while it has broadened what can be accomplished with a Platform-as-a-Service, CloudBees is still limited to just one technology.

Summary: Where Do You Want to Live?

With a portable Platform-as-a-Service, the major advantage is that you can take existing code and deploy it more easily, without major rewrites. It can be a faster iteration. If you need to move your application from a particular system into another environment, it generally takes a lot less effort.

The advantages of a non-portable platform are highly dependent on what that platform provides. For example, in Google App Engine, the advantage is tying into the infrastructure and operations of Google. In the case of Windows Azure, the advantage is tying into the operations of Microsoft.

The trade-offs depend on what kind of application you want to run. For example, if you need to run a Node.js application, you won't be able to do so on Google App Engine. But if you want to try Google's table functions, you won't be able to do that on Heroku or AppFog. Your selection of a portable or non-portable PaaS depends on your needs and what feature set you want to take advantage of. When all is said and done, however, you should keep your mind on what's down the road for your application; ultimately, you must ask yourself how much you are concerned about future changes to your code and where you want it to live.

Dealing with Legacy and Greenfield Apps

Another important consideration arises when you are evaluating PaaS options: are you moving existing applications or creating new ones? When answering that question, it is very important to think about the portable and non-portable aspects of Platform-as-a-Service.

If you have already written your code, it's going to be substantially more difficult to move your code into a non-portable Platform-as-a-Service. Rearchitecting a complex Python application in order for it to work on Google App Engine is going to be a much bigger challenge than trying to get it to run on AppFog or Cloud Foundry. In the case of Cloud Foundry, it could work right out of the box. In the case of Google App Engine, it may take significant engineering resources.

If you are creating new applications—if you want to start from scratch and if you have flexibility in terms of the language and technology choices you make—you'll have more choices in your selection of a platform. If you are evaluating technologies for scalability and performance, taking a look at Google App Engine and Windows Azure is very much worthwhile. If taking advantage of Google's operations and infrastructure would be advantageous to your greenfield application, it makes sense to try Google App Engine. The caveat is to think ahead and make sure that should something drastic happen to the platform you choose, you won't have boxed yourself into a corner.

An additional factor is pricing. If you are on a non-portable platform and the pricing changes, suddenly becoming too expensive, moving your application to another provider can be much more difficult than with a portable service.

One more issue: downtime. Almost every Platform-as-a-Service has had issues with reliability at some point. If your application can only run on one of these platforms, you take the risk that it will go down with that platform at some point. If your app is built more generically and can run on many different portable platforms, you can take advantage of that should you encounter reliability issues.

Tapping Into Services

Earlier, we briefly discussed services in the context of Heroku and Cloud Foundry. One of the big benefits of using a Platform-as-a-Service is the ability to tie quickly and easily into services such as MySQL, memcached, and PostgreSQL. There are a number of related advantages: you can get started with them quickly, they are managed and maintained for you, and typically the platform will do backups and provide redundancy.

There are disadvantages as well. On some platforms, it can be difficult to access your data and have an insight into the running of the services. And some services, especially those in the SQL family, are notorious for being difficult to scale. When your application grows, one of the biggest concerns is making sure that you have insight into your database systems; you want to be able to inspect all the details about how your code is interacting with your database and gain insight into how you can optimize your database accordingly.

It's a trade-off. On the one hand, you may experience lack of control. On the other hand, there is a huge advantage: automatic management.

The services model can play an important role when it comes to email. Functions such as sending email can be extremely difficult because email hosting providers have become very adept at sending mail to spam and junk mailboxes. They are accustomed to knowing when cloud providers are sending email and blocking it. This problem arises because spammers are able to spin many servers in the cloud very quickly in order to send massive amounts of email. So, many cloud providers are blacklisted. You are not allowed to send email, even if you try, which creates big problems when you are trying to create applications that send email. Luckily, integration with mailing systems within the services model lets you quickly tie into hosted mail senders who have solved these problems for you and have been approved explicitly by Gmail, Hotmail, and many email spam filters to let their messages go through. Doing that on your own is a very difficult task; having easy tie-ins to be able to do that through a hosted provider who is already whitelisted is a big advantage when you are creating applications.

Moving Toward Open Standards

Open standards are an important concept for Platform-as-a-Service because they can give a developer confidence about how to deploy an application independently of which service provider is doing it.

Having to learn the ins and outs of every single different provider can be a complete nightmare. However, we have already seen the wide variety of PaaS options out there and the different types of services that they provide.

The non-portable Platform-as-a-Service that started out with the simple premise of "We will give you the power of Google for your web application" provides a different solution than a portable platform like Heroku that says, "We will run the application without changing your code." And that is a much different type of solution than one that says, "We will give you your own Platform-as-a-Service that you can run on your laptop." Each of these providers has tried to tackle different problems and has a much different way of thinking about the way you create and deploy applications, which is why each has a different standard, a different feel, and a different look. They might use git-based deployment mechanisms, REST APIs, or proprietary systems for deploying. One might support continuous integration and one might focus on deployment. With such a variety, it has been hard to standardize on a single one.

The Allure of Open Source

Although historically there have been many different types of Platform-as-a-Service technologies, with more being born every day, there is the possibility for an emerging standard to appear around Cloud Foundry or OpenShift, a few of the open source options for PaaS.

There are several compelling reasons for this. The fact that you can run these technologies from your laptop is very compelling for developers trying to incorporate PaaS into their daily workflow. The other big plus for open source communities around PaaS is the fact that you can theoretically have choice between various providers with compatible PaaS options, or even run it yourself in production. In contrast, unless

Heroku open sources its technology stack, you are tied to Heroku's choice of infrastructure provider.

Taken together, these assets of open source PaaS offer an opportunity to create a standard around their APIs without the ability to lock anybody into a specific infrastructure or service provider. It also acts as an emerging standard for how to deploy applications in a standard way across infrastructures, both public and private.

We have already seen the start of using the Cloud Foundry API as a standard. AppFog uses it to deploy applications across Amazon Web Services, Rackspace, HP Cloud, and Windows Azure, which illustrates that one standard API can be used across different backends. The way that the developer interacts with these systems is though the Cloud Foundry API, decoupling the infrastructure implementation underneath from the API language that the developer uses to speak to it.

More and more PaaS technology is being open sourced every day. Cloud Foundry was one of the early leaders to do so, but Red Hat later open sourced OpenShift, GigaSpaces has an open source Cloudify offering, and even dotCloud has open sourced large chunks of its PaaS technology stack.

Evaluating Your Legacy

As you can see, there are a variety of PaaS providers out there, built for different needs and with different ideas in mind. When thinking about legacy applications and moving them to the cloud, it's a good idea to understand the limitations of the platforms with respect to the needs of your applications. In the next chapter, we'll take a deeper look at moving legacy apps to PaaS and provide solutions for some of the challenges you might encounter.

CHAPTER 4

Moving Legacy Apps to PaaS

Everyone has skeletons in their closets. Skeletons come in the form of technical debt, the applications written in Cobol, the spaghetti code that we always meant to clean up, that undocumented application that a coworker wrote before leaving, and all those applications that have been around for 10 years and nobody knows how they work anymore. These are commonly called *legacy applications*.

Developing apps in the cloud requires a new worldview and often adds a few different programming paradigms. While legacy applications can be adapted to work within PaaS, there is a common set of challenges to make them run well.

Fortunately, the changes needed to run your legacy apps in PaaS are also known as best practices today. These are the same changes you would need to make to your app if you just wanted to make it more reliable and robust, whether or not you ran it on a PaaS.

Initial Considerations

When you're developing applications for the cloud, there are certain assumptions you need to be aware of. This is true whether you're developing on IaaS or PaaS.

If you're deploying legacy apps to IaaS, the main benefit is the ability to provision virtual machines faster. The downside is that the virtual machines are usually ephemeral: they can go down; they're not typically reliable or robust. This forces you into thinking about building an application in a way that can be redundant, with your app running across many different servers.

This way of thinking is different from that in shared or dedicated hosting environments, where you assume that servers do not typically go down. In non-virtualized environments, one can often run an application with all of its services on a single server. Larger applications may put the database services on a separate machine. Frequently, there is no need to deal with replication issues, data consistency issues, or session management issues. When users upload code to these systems, the implicit assumption is that it's only on one server. This doesn't hold true when you have to build systems across many different servers.

Sidestepping Potential Problems

When working with IaaS, one has to assume that any server could go down at any minute, as they often do. PaaS offerings, which are typically built on IaaS, have usually thought out some of these potential problems for you. Building out N-tier application logic can be hard, and that is why PaaS can be so valuable; N-tier is built into PaaS from the start.

With PaaS, you don't have to figure out how to configure Apache on 20 different servers; you don't have to figure out how to load balance across those servers; you don't have to worry about MySQL slaves and master-master replication. Nor do you need to be concerned about redundancy, heartbeats, and failovers, as you would with IaaS.

However, with PaaS, you still have to write your code with the assumption that any individual instance of your app may go down at any moment. That forces you to think about building applications in a way that isn't consistent with some of the traditional methods of web development, especially for legacy applications. You will also need to take into consideration frameworks and content management systems (WordPress, Drupal, Joomla!) that haven't yet gotten up to speed with this new way of thinking and haven't yet incorporated ways to manage multi-instance applications.

We will cover specific examples of how to address these problems later in this chapter.

You have to make those changes yourself, and you have to start thinking not only about how your application will act if a few or even many of your instances go down, but also about how your application will act if the filesystem is not consistent across different instances.

Common Questions to Ask Yourself

Here are some common questions you will need to think about for legacy applications as related to the hard drive:

- If you can't rely on the hard drive being persistent or consistent, what does that mean for your application?
- If you're uploading content, where does it go? Where does it stay?
- What other assumptions does your application make about the hard drive?
- Where are your sessions kept? Many times, session state is held on the hard drive, and if you're running tens, dozens, or hundreds of instances, what does that mean from a user perspective?

- Are users going to stay logged in every time they hit the web page or is it going to log them out between visits?

Even More Legacy Code Issues

Another consideration when moving to PaaS is long-running processes. In traditional development methodology, there has rarely been a problem with long-running processes operating sequentially. Your application typically will just take longer to load, using a large amount of processing power up front, but this can be hidden behind the scenes with Ajax or some other frontend gimmicks. However, when you utilize PaaS, you have to think about long-running processes differently. In PaaS, long-running processes should be processed independently and are asynchronous from your main application logic. In fact, some PaaS providers enforce this by killing your main application if it runs for too long. Not all legacy applications were created to work that way.

These are just a few of the ways in which traditional development paradigms have evolved and how cloud paradigms are much different than the original ones. Now let's put those ideas into specific contexts.

Overview

What follows in this chapter is a set of the most common things you need to think about to transition legacy applications into PaaS. They are broken out into the following sections:

Asset Hosting
   How do you deal with uploaded content (images/videos/music)?

Session Management
   How do you deal with session data?

Caching
   How do you incorporate modern caching techniques?

Asynchronous Processing
   How do you handle long-running processes?

SQL
   What considerations are there for SQL in PaaS?

NoSQL
   How can you take advantage of modern trends of NoSQL?

Miscellaneous Gotchas

Asset Hosting

When users upload their content, whether it's a profile image, a movie, an attachment, or any kind of file, it is considered an *asset*. Traditionally, it hasn't been a problem to host those assets locally to the application (on the hard drive), since if the server crashes, you can restart it and your files will remain persisted. In modern cloud hosting, this assumption is no longer true. If a server crashes, depending on your IaaS or PaaS provider, the filesystem is often ephemeral and will not be restored on restart.

With many application platforms hosted in the cloud, IaaS or PaaS, when you restart your application or systems, you lose your uploaded content.

The upside to this is that new instances of your app are very easy to spin up; this is an essential piece of building on PaaS. However, it means that dealing with uploaded content in a way that's better and more robust becomes not only a good idea but also a necessary idea for developing applications. It's one of the first things you have to deal with when you're moving your legacy application into PaaS.

In terms of asset hosting, when you're dealing with a legacy application or a content management system like WordPress or Drupal, you're dealing with systems that tend to store items on the disk and in a specific file format. So, the challenges depend on whether you are taking an existing application built from scratch and turning that into a modern cloud application for PaaS, or trying to host WordPress, Drupal, or other CMS sites in the cloud. If you're doing the former, the general process is to use a blob storage system, also known as object storage.

All About Blob

There are two essential kinds of storage for assets: blob (binary large object) storage, also known as object storage, and file storage. *File storage* is the familiar kind of storage system used in traditional development. *Blob storage* works differently. Blobs are more like a key/value store for files, and are accessed through APIs like Amazon S3, Windows Azure Blob Storage, Google Cloud Storage, Rackspace Cloud Files, or OpenStack Swift.

When a user uploads assets to your application, a temporary file is usually created and moved to a more permanent location in the filesystem. When using blob storage, instead of moving files to a folder, you upload the asset to its final location (usually through a REST API) and are given a unique URL to reference the asset from. Once it's uploaded into the object storage mechanism, the API will give back the URL for that asset, at which point you can store the URL. Instead of storing the object on the disk, you now have a URL that you can reference; it's been uploaded into a persistent storage mechanism.

One of the benefits of using an object storage system is that all those files that were uploaded are automatically replicated on many different servers (up to seven or eight different copies will exist in many different parts of the world). It's very difficult to lose data and it's much more persistent; the content is much less likely to suffer damage based on any disk failure. You don't have to worry about backups as acutely as you would if your data were uploaded to your local disk.

There are even more added benefits depending on which object storage you use. Content delivery networks (CDNs) can speed up the delivery of your assets so that not only are they hosted in many different locations, but also, depending on where in the world you are, they can be served to you from the one that's closest to you. This can make the whole experience of consuming your assets and downloading the web pages feel a lot faster.

Because of the redundancy and CDN considerations, blob storage is a good idea in general, but it also has the added benefit of providing more speed, reliability, and robustness to your website. And it's not too difficult to implement. As you'll see in these code examples, the amount of effort that's required up front to deal with asset hosting is more than worth the investment in terms of what you get out of it.

PHP with Amazon S3

Amazon has libraries for using S3 in Ruby, Java, Python, .NET, and mobile phones. Here is an example of how easy S3 is to integrate with a PHP application. This code will not work out of the box because it only contains the relevant snippets for understanding the flow of code. To get code that is fully ready to go, you will need to go to Amazon's Sample Code & Libraries page (*http://aws.amazon.com/code/*), which has more detailed instructions for how to use the code. However, for the purposes of illustration, once the library is incorporated into your application it is not difficult to use:

```php
<?php
// S3.php is available from Amazon's AWS website
if (!class_exists('S3')) require_once('S3.php');

// Amazon gives you credentials if registered for S3
// Best practice is to make these ENV vars in a PaaS
$s3 = new S3(
    getenv("AWS_ACCESS_KEY"),
    getenv("AWS_SECRET_KEY")
);

// A "bucket" is analogous to the name of a folder
// It is a way to collect similar things together
$bucket = "MyPaaSAppBucket";

// Create the bucket
$s3->putBucket($bucket, S3::ACL_PUBLIC_READ);

// Assuming the file is POST'ed as a form element
// called "file", <input type="file" name="file" />
```

```
// Name the uploaded file. Bad idea to pass the name
// like this without any validation.
$file_name = $_FILES['file']['name'];

// Upload the file
$s3->putObjectFile(
    $_FILES['file']['tmp_name'],
    $bucket,
    $file_name,
    S3::ACL_PUBLIC_READ
);

$url = 'http://'.$bucket.'.s3.amazonaws.com/'.$file_name;
```

Node.js with Azure Blob Service

Like Amazon, Microsoft has libraries for using its Blob service in Ruby, Java, .NET, Python, PHP, and mobile phones. Here is an example of how easy Azure Blob is to integrate with a Node.js application. Again, this code will not work out of the box; you will need to go to Microsoft Azure's website (*http://www.windowsazure.com/en-us/ develop/*) for the code you need and more detailed instructions for how to use it. However, for illustration purposes, once the library is incorporated into your application it is not difficult to use:

```
// Azure in Node is available from npm install azure
var azure = require('azure');

// Azure gives you credentials if registered for blob
// Best practice is to make these ENV vars in a PaaS
// They will be called AZURE_STORAGE_ACCOUNT and
// AZURE_STORAGE_ACCESS_KEY

// Create a service and container to gather assets
var containerName = "myPaaSContainer";
var blobService = azure.createBlobService();
var container = blobService.createContainerIfNotExists(
    containerName,
    function(error){
        if(!error){
            // Container exists and is private
        }
    }
);

// The name of the uploaded object
var blobName = "myimage";

// The file name, possibly the uploaded temp file
var fileName = "/path/to/myimage.jpeg";

var blob = blobService.createBlockBlobFromFile(
```

```
          containerName,
          blobName,
          fileName,
              function(error){
                if(!error){
                    // File has been uploaded
                }
          }
);

var url =
  "http://"  + AZURE_STORAGE_ACCOUNT + ".blob.core.windows.net/" +
        containerName + "/" + blobName;
```

Generalized Asset Hosting Functions in Ruby for Rackspace Cloud Files

When integrating any blob functionality into your application, you will typically be doing various functions repeatedly, like uploading files and returning their corresponding URLs for storage in your database. To achieve maximum portability, it generally makes sense to add a layer of abstraction around this often-used code. That way, if you want to use a different object storage provider in the future, you can change your code mainly in one place rather than many.

You may organize these functions in a class if you are using an object-oriented language, or you may simply have some basic functions accessed globally.

The simple example class that follows is written in object-oriented Ruby. It contains some basic logic for working with Rackspace Cloud Files (*http://www.rackspace.com/cloud/files/*), but it could easily be ported to S3, Azure Blob, or any other object storage without affecting code that depends on it.

There are some libraries, such as Fog (*http://fog.io/storage/*), that have this logic already encapsulated in them:

```
// Usage: o = ObjectStorage.new(container_name)
//        o.upload(file, blob_name)
//        return o.url
class ObjectStorage
    def initialize(name)
        @@connection ||= CloudFiles::Connection.new(
            :username => ENV["USERNAME"],
            :api_key => ENV["API_KEY"]
        )
        @container = @@connection.container(name)
    end

    def upload(file, blob_name)
        @object = @container.create_object(blob_name, false)
        @object.write(file)
    end
```

```
    def url
        @object.public_url
    end
end
```

Uploading with Plug-ins

When you're dealing with a content management system (CMS), the process can be different. Systems like WordPress, Drupal, and Joomla! have plug-ins. Instead of rewriting code, you can install a plug-in, which may directly tie into blob services like S3. The plug-in upload mechanism stores the files directly into object storage and gives you back a URL. This improves the speed of the load time for your blog or CMS. Even better, it gives you a more scalable blog to which you can add more instances. When you load balance it to an instance that doesn't have the uploaded content, you'll never see the nefarious Error 404.

The following is a list of selected starting points for some of the most popular CMSs today. These URLs will have the latest code and documentation that will allow you to integrate with your applications quickly and easily:

WordPress plug-ins
- UpdraftPlus Backup (*http://wordpress.org/extend/plugins/updraftplus/*)
- CDN Sync Tool (*http://wordpress.org/extend/plugins/cdn-sync-tool/*)
- Amazon S3 Uploads (*http://bit.ly/130xAoz*)

Drupal modules
- Storage API (*http://drupal.org/project/storage_api*)
- Amazon S3 (*http://drupal.org/project/amazon_s3*)
- Cloud Files (*http://drupal.org/project/cloud_files*)
- S3 Auto Pushing (*http://drupal.org/project/s3autopush*)

Joomla! plug-ins
- JA Amazon S3 (*http://tinyurl.com/ja-amazon-s3*)
- jomCDN (*http://tinyurl.com/jomcdn*)

Session Management

Sessions are incredibly important to think about when scaling applications in PaaS. Unless configured otherwise, sessions are by default almost always stored in a temporary file on the hard drive. This is fine if your application only runs on one server, but with PaaS you can easily start many instances of your app, which means that it can be running on many different servers. To users of your app, this can end up making it look like they've suddenly been logged out randomly and for no reason.

A session is created, sometimes automatically (e.g., in PHP and Rails), by creating a unique random token. For the sake of explanation, let's say the token is XYZTOKEN and is stored in a cookie called MYAPP_SESSION_ID. Your PHP application will automatically know to look for a cookie named MYAPP_SESSION_ID, and if it finds that cookie, it takes the value and looks for the file corresponding to that token value. Again for simplification, let's say there is a directory in */tmp* called *phpsessions* and the token is a simple one-to-one relationship. Any arbitrary data for that user will then be saved in a hash and persisted to the file */tmp/phpsessions/XYZTOKEN*. This is an insecure simplification of what really happens, but it is a good illustration of the overall process.

If you are running your application on many different servers, you cannot depend on the filesystem to be the same on all of them. Therefore, you need to store session data in a different way.

With PaaS, there are three typical places you can store sessions. There are pros and cons to each type of session management:

Encrypted cookies for sessions
- Examples: default mechanism in Rails, plug-ins available for many other frameworks
- Pros: very fast and no need to run any external services
- Cons: limited amount of data can be stored, not available for every web framework

NoSQL storage for sessions
- Examples: memcached, MongoDB
- Pros: fast, you can store as much data as you want, supported by most frameworks
- Cons: dependency on external services that you may not use for anything but sessions

SQL storage for sessions
- Examples: MySQL, PostgreSQL
- Pros: you can utilize the same SQL database you are using within your applications already
- Cons: slower than the other two alternatives

There are many ways to implement these session management tools. They are highly dependent on the technology and framework you choose to develop with.

PHP

In PHP, you can overwrite the session handler to use any technology you want through the session_set_save_handler() function (*http://bit.ly/1bOzTSy*). If you are using the Zend Framework, there is a simple way to connect sessions to a database like MySQL using Zend_Session_SaveHandler_DbTable (*http://bit.ly/1axFE5B*). Other PHP frameworks have similar functionality built in, or you can write code yourself that will accomplish it pretty easily. Here is an annotated example from the PHP documentation for how to write sessions to files:

```php
<?php
class MySessionHandler implements SessionHandlerInterface
{
    private $savePath; // where to save session files

    // initialize the session object and create a directory
    // for session files if necessary
    public function open($savePath, $sessionName)
    {
        $this->savePath = $savePath;
        if (!is_dir($this->savePath)) {
            mkdir($this->savePath, 0777);
        }
        return true;
    }
    // no need to do anything when you close out a session
    // object
    public function close()
    {
        return true;
    }
    // for any given session id ($id) return the data
    // stored in the session file on disk
    public function read($id)
    {
        return (string) @file_get_contents("$this->savePath/sess_$id");
    }
    // write session data to a session file
    public function write($id, $data)
    {
        return file_put_contents("$this->savePath/sess_$id", $data) === false ?
        false : true;
    }
    // when you want to delete a session, delete the
    // session file containing the data
    public function destroy($id)
    {
        $file = "$this->savePath/sess_$id";
        if (file_exists($file)) {
            unlink($file);
        }
```

```
            return true;
    }
    // garbage collect sessions objects older than a given
    // amount of time
    public function gc($maxlifetime)
    {
        foreach (glob("$this->savePath/sess_*") as $file) {
            if (filemtime($file) + $maxlifetime < time() && file_exists($file)) {
                unlink($file);
            }
        }

        return true;
    }
}

$handler = new MySessionHandler();
session_set_save_handler($handler, true);
session_start();

// proceed to set and retrieve values by key from $_SESSION
```

Node.js

In Node.js, encrypted cookies can be implemented using a variety of npm modules. If you use the Connect middleware, *galette* and *cookie-sessions* are two plug-ins that give you encrypted cookie functionality.

Ruby

In Rails, the default session mechanism is an encrypted cookie, but if you want to change it to a Mongo or MySQL service all you have to do is edit *config/initializers/session_store.rb*.

Java

In Java, Tomcat has built-in clustering capabilities, where every session is replicated automatically to every Tomcat instance. This can be nice because enabling it does not require significant code changes; however, the downside is that managing and maintaining session replication can turn into a network overhead in this implementation and this Tomcat feature requires sticky sessions in the load balancer, which not every PaaS enables. If you want to try using encrypted cookies in Java, take a look at Marc Fasel's SessionInCookie application (*https://github.com/marcfasel/SessionInCookie*) and the associated blog post (*http://bit.ly/197Y1A2*), which has more details.

Caching

Caching is a very important part of making web architecture scalable, and it can take many different forms.

A brute but effective form of caching is to take dynamic content that's generated server-side, download it as a file onto the disk, and then serve that file from disk. Caching to disk can minimize CPU turnaround for each request, making it extremely fast; it can increase the number of requests per second that can be made on your website by orders of magnitude. Cached data can also be stored in RAM or NoSQL, which removes even more latency from this process and makes it more scalable across instances of your application.

Alternatively, another caching technique is to take fragments of the generated code and store them in RAM or a NoSQL cache. If used correctly, this technique can also increase the speed of your website by an order of magnitude, creating a blend of dynamic and static content mixing speed with power.

Depending on the language you are writing code in, it is often also possible to precompile source code. In PHP, you'll find solutions like APC or bytecode generation that will increase the performance of your application by preparsing and preunderstanding the code that's going to be run. In Java compilation is a necessary step, so this does not apply, but for many dynamic languages (like Python and Node.js) there is added value in a precompiled cache step.

Filling In the Pieces

Depending on individual circumstances, caching is a technology that may not need to be migrated from your legacy application into your cloud-based PaaS in order for you to move forward. Why? Because often caching is built in such a way that if a piece of HTML is missing—if it doesn't exist on the disk, or doesn't exist where it is expected to be—the system will compensate by regenerating the correct content.

For example, if you have three different instances of your code and the cache has only been populated to disk on one of those instances, when you happen to hit an instance that doesn't have a cache yet the system will generate that code and then save it to the second instance; the next time a request comes in to the second instance, it won't have to be generated again.

The biggest downside to relying on this is that it can lead to situations where a user sees different content when reloading a cached page. If one instance has a copy that was made a week ago and another has a copy made three days ago and another copy is fresh, every reload may present different information.

However, this is not always a problem, so from a caching perspective, migrating a legacy app is not necessarily going to create a poor user experience. However, anytime you put something on a disk, that disk can crash, or data might not be consistent across all the disks; what might be cached on one server might be different from what's cached on another, which could result in an inconsistent user experience.

When moving legacy applications to PaaS, you can use the opportunity to implement best practices and create a central cache storage for your application, using SQL or NoSQL databases to store that data instead of a disk. So, instead of making calls to disk, you can use technology like memcached, Redis, MongoDB, or CouchDB. In some cases, you might cache the data directly into a SQL database, putting it into MySQL or PostgreSQL.

With the MySQL and PostgreSQL options, the upside is that you usually already have connections to your database that you can use and you don't need external dependencies on yet another service. So if you're not using memcached or another NoSQL service in your application, it may make more sense to simply use your MySQL database, since you already are using that for other aspects of your app. However, as you're looking more and more into performance and scalability, the benefits of using memcached and other NoSQL value stores will become clear: much of the time data can be extracted far faster, especially with memcached. In NoSQL, you are usually storing that data right in the RAM, and that's the fastest place to get it. In most SQL databases, frequently used data is also kept in RAM to an extent. If your databases do not exceed the limits of how much data is cached in RAM, you may not see a substantial difference using memcached or MySQL. However, as your datasets grow, this may become a bottleneck down the road.

One of the great benefits to using PaaS is how simple it is to add more services to your application as well. For example, if you were afraid of using MongoDB because you did not want to run and scale it, PaaS will do that for you, so you have more flexibility to try services that you otherwise might have stayed away from.

Caching with memcached in PHP

Implementing client-side integration with caching is generally a very easy process. In PHP, if you are on Ubuntu, all you need to do is run sudo apt-get install php5-memcached to install the client memcached libraries for PHP. Then you can use the following code to get and set values in the memcached key/value store:

```php
<?php
$cache = new Memcached();

// memcached allows multiple servers, best to
// keep the names in environment variables
$cache->addServer(
    getenv("MEMCACHED_SERVER"), getenv("MEMCACHED_PORT")
);

// set
```

```
$cache->set("foo", "Hello World!");

// get
$cache->get("foo"),
?>
```

Caching with MongoDB in Node.js

Caching with a NoSQL database like MongoDB is generally as easy to do as using a
simple RAM hash system like memcached. This is because essentially, these are all basically key/value stores and caching is a primitive form of distributed key/value storage.
(This is not completely true, especially when it comes to expiration of key/value pairs,
but it can naively be treated as such for most uses.)

In Node.js, there is an npm module called *mongodb* that provides a *mongodb* client.
Simply running npm install mongodb will install it:

```
// pass the connection string in through env vars
var mongourl = process.env.ENV_VARIABLE["mongourl"];
require('mongodb').connect(mongourl, function(err, cache) {
    var collection = db.collection('cache');

    // set
    collection.insert({
        key: "foo",
        value: "Hello World!"
    });

    // get
    collection.findOne({ key: "foo" },
        function(err, item) {}
    );
});
```

Generalized Caching Functions in Ruby for Redis

When integrating any caching functionality into your application, you will typically be
doing various functions repeatedly, like getting and setting key/value pairs. For maximum portability, it generally makes sense to add a layer of abstraction around this often-
used code. That way, if you want to use a different object storage provider in the future,
you can change your code mainly in one place rather than many.

You may organize these functions in a class if you are using an object-oriented language,
or you may simply have some basic functions accessed globally.

The simple example class that follows is written in object-oriented Ruby. It contains
some basic logic for working with Redis but could easily be ported to MySQL,
memcached, or any other technology that can be used with caching:

```
gem "redis"
require "redis"

// Usage: cache = ObjectCache.new
//        cache["key"] = "value"
//        return cache["key"]
class ObjectCache
    def initialize
        @connection = Redis.new(
            ENV["REDIS_SERVER"]
        )
    end

    def [](key)
        @connection[key]
    end

    def []=(key, value)
        @connection[key] = value
    end
end
```

Asynchronous Processing

Long-running tasks—tasks that take a lot of CPU, RAM, or processing power—should be moved into the background so that they don't affect the user's experience on a website. Platform-as-a-Service providers will often kill long-running web-facing processes. This makes asynchronous processing a requirement rather than simply a best practice for moving legacy applications to the cloud.

Serving Up Stored Data

Here's an example. You have a long list of data, maybe RSS URLs. This data is processed through many high-latency API calls (regularly polling RSS feeds from various sources). Because that data needs to be presented very quickly, you don't want to be gathering it while processing queries in real time as the user is viewing the data.

Another example is processing images or videos. When you're uploading an image, an application may want to resize it, compress it, or do any number of other tasks. Depending on the size of that image, processing it can take a large amount of RAM, CPU, and time. The processing can take a long time (minutes or even hours), and a user of your application should not have to wait for your application to process the data in real time. Processing images and videos should be done asynchronously and the result should be pushed to the user as the processing finishes.

To accomplish this, you need asynchronous processes that will gather and calculate in the background, using as much time and as much CPU as needed. The data can be stored either in the database or in your caching mechanism. Once stored, it can be accessed quickly and directly in real time from the web frontend application.

How to Create Asynchronous Processes

The generic technique for setting up long-running processes is actually quite simple. Here is some pseudocode for before:

```
for each task in tasks
do
    // could take a while
    process the task
end
```

and after:

```
for each task in tasks
do
    // only takes a millisecond
    queue task for processing
end
```

The processing code will look like this:

```
loop
do
    grab task from queue
    process the task
end
```

More Advanced Scheduling of Background Tasks

As you become more familiar with incorporating background processing into your applications, you may want to get fancier with it. You can incorporate open source systems like Celery (*http://www.celeryproject.org/*) for Python, which provides an asynchronous task queue based on distributed message passing and also supports scheduling tasks at certain times. Celery uses RabbitMQ, Redis, Beanstalk, MongoDB, or CouchDB as a backend for its service.

In Ruby, there is a similar project called Resque (*https://github.com/defunkt/resque*) backed by Redis (*https://github.com/blog/542-introducing-resque*). These projects have the added flexibility of giving insight into the health and state of your queue, which is critical as the scale of your applications grow.

Aside from open source projects, there are even some third-party services that specialize in background tasks, like Iron.io's IronWorker (*http://www.iron.io/worker*). IronWorker has libraries in Ruby, Python, PHP, Node.js, Go, Java, and .NET, and unlike Celery it does not require you to have any integration with a service like RabbitMQ or Redis. It is a fully managed service that takes your processing code and runs it for you in the cloud on servers managed by Iron.io.

SQL

When you're dealing with legacy applications and looking to move them into PaaS, it is important to be aware of the abilities and limitations of the SQL services provided by the platforms that are available to you.

The Dilemma of Stored Procedures

A common "gotcha" in dealing with databases from legacy systems is stored procedures. The problem with stored procedures is that they can be used pretty commonly within legacy applications. However, in many platforms, the hosted databases are not very friendly to stored procedures; with many PaaS providers, they are completely disabled, which can be a problem for legacy applications. It is usually not considered a best practice to use stored procedures; although they have been used in the past, the modern programming methodologies discourage their use.

Stored procedures are functions stored in the database itself that can be used as first-class citizens when doing SQL queries on that database. A trivial example of a stored procedure might be adding two columns together on a database; you can select that stored procedure and get the combination of those columns without having to do the processing in your code.

Of course, stored procedures can get a lot more complicated and offset much of the computational effort of processing data into the database instead of the code.

One of the big problems with stored procedures is that they create one-offs that are hard to remember and hard to keep track of. It is hard to remember what stored procedures are used and need to be maintained, which makes code harder to debug and especially hard to run tests against. When you are running a local version of the database—in addition to a QA version, a development version, and a production version—it is incredibly difficult and untenable to maintain, distribute, and change stored procedures across all of them all the time. The rise of unit testing was one of the nails in the coffin of stored procedures. The inability to easily and effectively run unit tests against stored procedures across all databases took them out of fashion.

If stored procedures are impossible to remove from your application, there are solutions. PaaS providers have started to look into third-party dedicated databases, and some even offer dedicated databases themselves. There are now providers that offer MySQL-as-a-Service on a dedicated basis, including Xeround and ClearDB. Even Amazon has a MySQL service called RDS, which is a dedicated and managed MySQL environment. Typically, when you have a dedicated MySQL instance, storing those procedures is allowed.

So, if you can't get around the dilemma of stored procedures, there are ways that you can still migrate your legacy applications into the cloud. However, the solutions can get expensive, and it might be harder to set up slaves and ensure consistency across multiple databases as you grow.

NoSQL

In legacy applications, NoSQL is one of the easier items to migrate into a PaaS, because there is no concept of stored procedures. There's very little overhead involved. It's a similar interface for most NoSQL services running within a PaaS; it runs just as easily as it would if you were outside of one. Whether your key/value storage is as simple as memcached or as robust as Riak, it will typically work very similarly within a cloud environment. In fact, a number of the NoSQL options can help you in many ways, such as with asset hosting, caching, and even asynchronous processing. Leveraging those key/value storages in various ways can actually help when you're moving your legacy applications into PaaS.

Here is an incomplete list of NoSQL databases that you can choose from:

- MongoDB
- CouchDB
- Redis
- Cassandra
- Riak
- HBase
- Cassandra
- Amazon SimpleDB
- Amazon DynamoDB
- Azure Table Storage

Miscellaneous Gotchas

When you're migrating any legacy application into PaaS, you must consider how your application will survive and how the user experience will look if the disk goes away or if any one individual server dies.

PaaS can deal with managing, load balancing, network failover, and heartbeat monitoring of your individual services. It can do much of the work for you, but it cannot rewrite your legacy code for you (yet). It cannot know the dependencies within your code that are related to writing to the disk. Many times there are small pieces of code in a library you have forgotten about that have assumptions regarding storing information. Trying to port and migrate your applications into PaaS can often feel like looking for a needle in a haystack. But once you have done so, the benefits are large and important: you are making your application conform to standards independent of cloud standards that are simply known throughout the industry as best practices.

When you are prototyping applications or building them in the early stages, you might never think that it's going to get to the point where you'll need to migrate to PaaS. This leads us to consider another gotcha.

The Optimization Trap

One of the easiest traps to fall into when writing or rewriting your code is premature optimization: building features that you think are going to be needed or optimizing aspects of your app before they actually need to be optimized. However, the topics and actions we have discussed so far in this chapter do not fall into the camp of premature optimization. They really fall into the category of best practices, because any application that starts to grow is always going to need to employ PaaS.

Premature optimization is making an optimization that may or may not matter at scale. All of the topics we've covered in this chapter will always matter, and should be considered when you're building your applications from scratch so that you don't end up having to port more legacy code somewhere down the line.

Starting from Scratch

Is it better just to throw out your legacy applications and start from scratch?

It depends. The considerations will be different for every application, for every developer, for every team. There are certainly going to be cases and situations where it makes more sense to redo your code from scratch. There will also be cases where you will not be able to do so, since you might be dependent on code from systems like WordPress or Drupal; you might be so dependent on legacy code that throwing it out and starting from scratch is simply not an option.

There are also cases in which an application has grown to a size that makes it very difficult to throw out all the existing code. Other projects that might have pieces of code that can be thrown out, enabling you to decouple and create smaller applications to do the services—file uploads, for example—independently of the main code itself. Again, it definitely depends on the situation.

A Final Note on Legacy Apps

Look for all the places where your code depends either directly on the disk or on any individual server. Consider storing in RAM data that is needed across many instances and auditing for every place that could possibly affect the user experience negatively.

CHAPTER 5

Writing New Apps for PaaS

Legacy web applications tended to be monolithic and difficult to scale. As we saw in Chapter 4, it's possible to move legacy applications to Platform-as-a-Service, but it can be tedious as the architecture is generally quite different. The true power of Platform-as-a-Service is realized when you start from scratch, writing new applications.

Before we take a look at creating new apps on PaaS, it will be useful to examine the monolithic nature of old-school applications.

Breaking Down the Monolith

Monolithic code is where you take one application and keep adding more capabilities to it, sticking on features and adding search functions, account management, and blog posts. It's a Frankenstein monster. It's a patchwork. You get memory leaks, and the app consumes more and more RAM.

Debugging these apps becomes a maze, whereas if each of your individual components is separate—i.e., if the search component is separate from the blog post component, which is separate from the user component, etc.—and each of those components can run and scale independently, you have much more flexibility. For example, if your service depends more highly on a search function than it does on managing and registering users, you can scale the search component up very high, giving it many resources, while on the other hand the user component can be a very small application. But if it's a monolithic application, every component is part of the big app.

Even if you start trying to rope off components of an application that you suspect have memory leaks by routing those requests to a separate pool of processes, that is about as effective as throwing a carpet over dry-rotted wood floors. The problem not only does not go away, but actually gets worse.

A best practice for programming and within Platform-as-a-Service is to think of each of your data sources and each of your application's areas of expertise as a small, independently running service. When you decompose monolithic applications into smaller ones that all are tied together and interact, the benefits of PaaS become clear very quickly.

Small applications that do one thing well are much easier to scale because you can pick different backend technologies that are right for the tool. In a large monolithic application, you might shove one backend technology into it simply because that's the technology used for everything else. You might use MySQL where Redis might be the better option, or you might use PostgreSQL where a MongoDB database might make more sense.

Debugging smaller applications is significantly easier as well. The more code there is within an individual application, the more interdependent the application becomes, making it harder to test because the interdependencies require testing more and more edge cases.

A best practice for professional developers is to constantly test their code, through unit, functional, and integration tests. This is also much easier to do with smaller, service-based applications than it is with a large interdependent monolith. With smaller services, you end up with components that can more easily be exhaustively and independently tested.

Programming history is littered with examples of large monolithic applications being built up and then torn apart, sometimes many times, over and over. Twitter started out in 2006 as a relatively monolithic Rails application. In 2010, it was decoupled into an API serving a lightweight JavaScript frontend (*http://tinyurl.com/twitter-decoupled*). Since then, it has added functionality in a service-oriented way, incorporating technologies like Scala and Python and even Drupal to create a highly distributed scalable system (*https://dev.twitter.com/opensource/thanks*). You can track the history of Twitter's adventures in breaking down the monolith at the High Scalability blog (*http://tinyurl.com/making-twitter-fast*). Eventually, Twitter replaced its JavaScript API–consuming frontend with a more dynamic frontend, for various reasons; however, the dynamic frontend still consumes the same distributed APIs underneath.

Similar stories can be found at many large and small companies today. Developers are starting to learn lessons from these large-scale services and to develop best practices around them, so that they can balance speed of development with an overall architecture better suited to the needs of scaling. It is essentially a reemergence of service-oriented architecture (SOA) for the Web using new technologies to make it easier to build and maintain, as well as standards (like REST) to make services more manageable and uniform.

Independent Thinking

Consider a common scenario for large businesses and financial or government institutions, where you're building an application that has data-constrained portions that can only run in house. This data-restricted part of your application usually ends up being a small fraction of the app, perhaps 5% to 10%.

If you build your application monolithically, the entire application will have to be run in house due to the data constraints. However, if you build it to run as a distributed system, with many APIs feeding into a lightweight JavaScript frontend, or even a simple dynamic frontend that consumes other service APIs, you can still host 90% of your application safely in the public cloud. All the mundane pieces that do not interact with sensitive data can be run on commodity hardware that is cheaper to run in the cloud.

We've seen many successful examples of this modern service-oriented, API-driven architecture. We already mentioned Twitter, but Gmail also took a very API-driven, client-side approach, putting together APIs that interact with the mail and having the frontend JavaScript client consume it all. Apple did something similar with MobileMe: the backends are simple APIs, and the frontend is a thick, client-side application that handles much of the logic in real time. This enables more flexibility, more scalability, and more foresight, leading to better, more maintainable applications.

This approach of building many smaller services works especially well with Platform-as-a-Service. In fact, it is a best practice to do it this way with PaaS. Making small independent services that all tie together on the frontend is not only a modern approach to developing both web and mobile applications, but also ties in well when you are trying to decide how to incorporate a Platform-as-a-Service strategy.

Leveraging APIs for Mobile Development

One of the driving motivations behind the decomposition and servicification of application development also happens to be one the biggest, most disruptive technologies that we face today: mobile technology. The mobile sphere has grown quickly to become a vital piece of our lives. In 2012, there were 54 billion cumulative downloads of native apps in app stores, adding more than 2 million downloads a month. Some estimates say that this represents only one-tenth of the entire market for mobile applications.

In a world where there are half a trillion mobile applications, the computing power and programming paradigms for systems supporting these applications will need to keep up. Many mobile applications are fed by backend services to register users; share photos, news, and information; offer advertisements; and provide many more dynamic features. Apps like Instagram, Pinterest, and even Facebook would be nothing without the backend API infrastructure to feed them.

One of the biggest success stories in recent mobile application development is Instagram (*http://instagram.com*). With a team of only 13 people, its creators built a billion-dollar company from a mobile application. What programming work were those 13 people actually doing? The native mobile application side of Instagram is not the most complex technology in the world. Significantly harder was building the backend to support the native mobile application for millions of concurrent users. Building the infrastructure underneath the mobile application to gather and share the information and process the photos was an incredibly difficult challenge. This team used the Amazon cloud to accomplish this feat. For more details about how they did it, you can read the High Scalability blog post, "The Instagram Architecture Facebook Bought For A Cool Billion Dollars" (*http://bit.ly/1aYFKqv*).

The success of Instagram is indicative of the potential for modern application developers, both in enterprises and in small startups, to get in front of millions, or even tens of millions, of smartphone users. However, you need to be prepared to manage and deal with the backend constraints that such a deluge of customers puts on your service. Those kinds of constraints make it necessary to build scalable API services.

The beauty of these services is that these APIs, if well constructed and well thought out, are exactly the same APIs that can power your modern web applications as well. If you approach building these applications from a service-oriented perspective, the services can be the backend for both your mobile and your web applications. If you think about building your web application this way from the start, when you are ready to add a mobile application, it is already prepared. It already has the same data sources for your mobile application to consume. If you have a mobile application and you need a web presence in front of it, this is a great way to leverage that kind of technology.

The Emergence of JSON and REST

In the early incarnations of service-oriented architecture, standards like SOAP, XML-RPC, and WSDL were common for structuring data and communicating through APIs. These were heavyweight and inflexible standards that were typically pretty hard to work with.

In the reemergence of service-oriented architecture, there are new, more nimble and lightweight concepts like JSON and REST, which enable agility and velocity while keeping the benefits of a loosely coupled distributed system.

A Look at JSON

JSON (short for JavaScript Object Notation) has emerged as a standard format for transferring data within API services, serving as an alternative to XML. JSON is used in a wide range of applications, including Gmail, MobileMe, iCloud, Twitter, LinkedIn, and almost every major website you're likely to interact with. One of the reasons that it has been so predominant is because it is easy and natural for JavaScript on the web frontends to consume the JSON data. JSON has strong support on native mobile clients as well. The great libraries for parsing JSON within mobile and web APIs have made it a natural standard for generating and presenting the data for modern application design.

The JSON scheme is not hard to read, both for computers and for humans. Here is an example:

```
{
    "id": 1,
    "name": "Programming for PaaS",
    "price": 123,
    "tags": ["PaaS", "Programming"]
}
```

One of the nice aspects of the JSON format is how easy it is for web browsers to parse. This makes it a great format for Ajax programming techniques. Here is an example of how easy it is for a native JavaScript client like the one in your browser or in any Node.js application to parse:

```
var object = eval(text);
```

This is not the most secure technique (validating the text before executing it is always best practice). However, it shows the power of the JSON format.

A Look at REST

REST (short for Representational State Transfer) is an architecture pattern (or style) for distributed systems like the Web. REST has become a predominant service design model, reusing HTTP's basic vocabulary like GET, POST, PUT, and DELETE. Because REST uses simple HTTP commands, it uses much less bandwidth than services like SOAP that demand lengthy headers and heavy XML parsing.

The basic principle behind REST is to provide a shared network vocabulary for transferring resources in a standard and predictable format. What does that mean? Let's look at an example of what a RESTful JSON service for serving and managing user data might look like:

GET
    Lists the resource (cacheable)

 • http://example.com/users[1]

        Header:
          none
        Response:

---

1. Limits and offsets can be sent as query strings and are helpful for paging large collections. For example: ?limit=2&offset=122.

```
[
 {'id': 123,
  'name': 'a'},
 {'id': 124,
  'name': 'b'}
]
```

- http://example.com/users/123

    Header:
      none
    Response:
    ```
    {'id': 123,
     'name': 'a'}
    ```

- http://example.com/users?name=b[2]

    Header:
      none
    Response:
    ```
    [
     {'id': 124,
      'name': 'b'}
    ]
    ```

PUT

Updates the resource (not cacheable)

- http://example.com/users

    Header:
    ```
    [
     {'id': 123,
      'name': 'x'},
     {'id': 124,
      'name': 'y'}
    ]
    ```
    Response:
      200 OK

- http://example.com/users/123

    Header:
    ```
    {'id': 123,
     'name': 'x'}
    ```
    Response:
      200 OK

- http://example.com/users?name=b

    Header:
    ```
    [
     {'id': 124,
    ```

2. This is how you do search RESTfully; limits and offsets can also be added.

```
              'name': 'y'}
          ]
        Response:
          200 OK
```

POST

Creates a new resource (not cacheable)

- http://example.com/users

  ```
    Header:
      {'id': 125,
       'name': 'c'}
    Response:
      200 OK
  ```

- http://example.com/users/123

  Not used

- http://example.com/users?name=b

  Query strings are not needed when creating new resources

DELETE

Removes the resource (not cacheable)

- http://example.com/users

  ```
    Header:
      None
    Response:
      200 OK
    Note:
      Deleted all users
  ```

- http://example.com/users/123

  ```
    Header:
      None
    Response:
      200 OK
    Note:
      Deleted only user 123
  ```

- http://example.com/users?name=b

  ```
    Header:
      None
    Response:
      200 OK
    Note:
      Deleted all users named b
  ```

With a RESTful approach, getting and managing services becomes predictable and straightforward. Creating and scaling any particular RESTful service is not usually very challenging.

For example, if your service is unlikely to get more than 100,000 rows in the next few years, then there is little need to worry about scaling beyond a traditional MySQL or PostgreSQL database table. These traditional SQL tables can easily scale to millions or even tens of millions of rows on a single server.

However, if you anticipate the service growing to 100,000,000 rows, you might want to consider a database better suited to highly distributed growth, like Riak or CouchDB.

A Look at Metaservices

A metaservice is a RESTful application for serving collections of data.

In slightly more detail, it is a lightweight application that consumes a core service (e.g., MySQL, MongoDB, Redis, memcached, etc.) and produces a REST API, which generally serves JSON or XML serialized data.

A metaservice is like a core service wrapped in REST with limited application logic specific to whatever the metaservice specializes in. Examples include a user registration metaservice, a commenting metaservice, a message metaservice, and a blog metaservice. Sometimes the same database serves various metaservices, but in other cases the metaservices will have their own databases and core services.

Traditionally, instead of building metaservices for data sources, you would build a lot of code that essentially did the functionality of REST, but mixed a bunch of services together, cross-function the logic, and, instead of generating simple JSON serialized objects, resulted in a complex mess of dynamically generated HTML, CSS, and Java-Script. When you wanted to swap out components, you found it difficult, if not impossible. When you wanted to scale components, they would be intertwined. The same table that would only need 100 records accessed frequently was on the same database as the one that needed to grow to 100,000,000 records, which would be infrequently accessed but needed to support fast indexed searching. This is the nightmare of scaling web applications in a traditional way—and it is a path that has been trodden by thousands of developers before you. Those developers usually ended up decomposing these applications into metaservices, so why not go with metaservices from the start?

A metaservice is built on top of the idea of a core service. It's powered by these services —by the MySQLs, MongoDBs, and PostgreSQLs of the world. However, they are wrapped within a lightweight API that can still talk directly to the drivers and services. Instead of presenting HTML, or a finished frontend to be delivered directly to the user, these are typically much simpler. They simply generate JSON: serialized data structures built on the existing services. So, a metaservice delivers serialized data to be consumed by the client frontend, typically using a serialization format like JSON. These metaservices have become the building blocks of modern, scalable web architecture.

There are frameworks well suited to quickly generating RESTful applications in every language you can think of. Chapter 10 has a full list of frameworks specifically built for a wide variety of languages. No matter what language you use, you should be able to find an appropriate REST framework.

The one thing all of these frameworks have in common is that they make it easy to develop RESTfully routed URLs and provide structure to the code that responds to each HTTP verb (GET, PUT, POST, DELETE, etc.).

Consuming RESTful Metaservices

Why use metaservices? Metaservices are very simple to build and simple to consume. They don't usually use as much logic as monolithic applications. That leads to getting work done faster.

Once they are created, metaservices can be consumed in multiple ways. They can be consumed on mobile clients or on the Web, and they can be put together using different technologies on the frontend.

Application Clients

There are many libraries in every programming language built to consume metaservices. You give the library a RESTful URL, and it will model the result for you in your code. This lets you stitch together many metaservices in a lightweight, dynamic backend that can serve the compiled data to the end user. Here is a code example using Ruby's ActiveResource library that shows an example of how easy these libraries can be to interact with:

```
class Person < ActiveResource::Base
    self.site = ENV["PEOPLE_REST_URL"] // Best Practice
end

ryan = Person.new(
    :first => 'Ryan',
    :last => 'Daigle'
)

ryan.save                # => true
ryan.id                  # => 2
Person.exists?(ryan.id)  # => true
ryan.exists?             # => true

ryan = Person.find(1)
# Resource holding our newly created Person object
```

```
ryan.first = 'Rizzle'
ryan.save               # => true

ryan.destroy            # => true
```

You can see how powerful REST clients can be. They can be consumed very similarly to core services like MySQL and PostgreSQL, and serve many more purposes as well.

Mobile Clients

This will be covered in Chapter 6.

Thin Web Clients

Metaservices can be consumed directly in the browser. In fact, you do not need any frameworks at all to process a standard RESTful URL. Any browser-based Ajax call with an exec() function can do the trick:

```
var url = "http://example.com/users";
var req = new XMLHttpRequest();

req.onreadystatechange = function() {
  if (req.status == 200) {
    var json = req.responseText;

    // this is not secure, only
    // showing this for example
    var object = exec(json);

    // do something with
    // the object...
  }
}

req.open("GET", url, true);
req.send();
```

This code can be a little tricky and cumbersome, but some really great modern JavaScript frameworks have been developed that you can add to any website that will not only automate the consumption of these metaservices, but also display the data in a structured way. They include:

- Backbone (*http://backbonejs.org/*)
- Angular (*http://angularjs.org/*)
- Ember (*http://emberjs.com/*)
- Spine (*http://spinejs.com/*)
- Knockout (*http://knockoutjs.com/*)

For a deeper discussion on how to select the proper JavaScript framework for your needs, see Steven Anderson's blog post, "Rich JavaScript Applications—the Seven Frameworks" (*http://bit.ly/18v52pw*).

Thick Web Clients

Impressive technologies like SproutCore (*http://sproutcore.com/*) and Cappuccino (*http://www.cappuccino-project.org/*) are able to provide building blocks to bind your data against. This is a well thought out and proven method for developing applications in modern desktop environments, incorporating data sources and data bindings.

As our JavaScript frontend client layers get thicker and thicker, we're starting to see more and more composition of data sources in the frontend. Frontends are being presented through very dynamic, well presented, structured web interfaces.

Tools like SproutCore and Cappuccino provide building blocks, the foundational pieces that are tied together in a very standard way to build modern applications that feel like desktop applications on your web or mobile clients. In fact, SproutCore and Cappuccino are similar to using Apple's Xcode or Microsoft's Visual Studio. To a traditional web developer who has never created a desktop or native mobile application before, these tools can feel strange at first. The visual components are more strictly defined for you, and once you bind data sources to them, they seem to magically just work.

One of the benefits of using these technologies is that they are so prescribed, they have such a strong experience tied into them, that some of these clients can actually be compiled into native mobile applications. If you write your application in Cappuccino, for example, there are services like NativeHost that will compile your application without having to change anything to run in a desktop environment as a native app, which leads to a cross-media way of thinking about application development.

These technologies are so rich and becoming so well supported that we are seeing even large companies starting to use them. Apple has used SproutCore to build out its entire iCloud suite of web applications, supporting Mail, Contacts, Calendar, Notes, Reminders, Find My Phone, and iWork. NPR has built a beautiful Cappuccino-based player to stream its radio content. There are many new examples of adoption of these thick client interfaces every day.

The Unique Contribution of PaaS

The weaknesses of migrating legacy applications into Platform-as-a-Service are exactly the kinds of weaknesses that are counterbalanced when you develop applications using metaservices.

In a monolithic app, you have to worry about all sorts of things, like which parts of your app are using the disk, where it is leaking memory, and what code is running where. It becomes very complicated to move legacy applications because there are simply so many components to them.

When you're using the new approaches listed in this chapter to develop applications, the benefits include the ability to build simpler, more lightweight backend clients that have less dependence on filesystems and more dependence on scalable services. It is much easier to add more instances of whatever part of your app needs to scale. Need more capacity on the search component of your site? Focus just on the search metaservice.

Using these best practices and developing an app from scratch, you're thinking about how each component can survive and scale independently; these are exactly the kinds of problems that you would need to solve when migrating an application from a monolith into Platform-as-a-Service. In fact, one of the most effective ways to migrate legacy code into PaaS is by separating logical chunks of your monolith into metaservices and starting to decompose your app piece by piece.

Four Important Benefits

This new form of development yields significant benefits in four important areas: agility, time to market, scalability, and interoperability.

Agility

Agility is being able to move quickly with the needs of an application. It's the ability to add new features. It's the ability to move features that aren't working out of the program and to rebuild features. Building applications for PaaS using a service-oriented metaservice approach increases that agility manyfold.

PaaS increases agility when you're adding features and functionality, because independent teams can be working on these metaservices independently. If you need to add functionality, you can do so without having to deconstruct and understand the entire monolith of your application. In short, Platform-as-a-Service lets you be much more agile when thinking about application deployment.

Time to market

Time to market is shorter with these new techniques. You spend less time thinking about maintaining and scaling an application, and much more time thinking about how all the components work together.

You are not spending time building up a huge monolith. You can prototype a simple backend, make sure that it works and is consumable on the frontend, and get your application up and running very quickly (much faster than if you had had to architect the entire system up front).

Scalability

It becomes much easier to scale an application if the pain points of the application can be limited to one or two different services that are the key components. If you break those out and they become independent of each other, if the data sources can be independent, you can think about the scalability of much smaller components, which turns out to be a much easier problem to solve.

Interoperability

One of the great benefits of building applications in this manner is that the frontend rarely cares where the services and metaservices are hosted, making it a generational leap forward in interoperability. In fact, an application can now be consumed from many different data sources, many different data centers, many different regions, and many different vendors. It becomes an interoperable patchwork of scalable modern architecture.

A Solution for Enterprises and Governments

One of the most vexing problems for enterprises and governments is how to realize the benefits of utilizing public cloud systems while keeping sensitive data restricted. Using the methods we've discussed in this chapter, businesses and governments can get the best of both worlds. They can enjoy the best agility and fastest time to market. They can utilize business-critical IT applications as services that are consumed in public cloud –hosted applications and mobile apps, which are delivered to their employees and customers in a safe and secure manner. This means they can start to experience the benefits that have already been realized by many smaller technology companies.

In addition, with metaservices, there can be independent teams working together in parallel on many different aspects of an application. Thus, tackling the development of large applications becomes a simpler problem of small teams focused on doing one thing very well.

The Effect of Moore's Law

The reason that client-side JavaScript and thick clients are becoming more popular isn't simply a matter of fashion. It is not simply the "cool" way to develop applications. It's actually driven by Moore's law. It's driven by the nature of computation itself.

In the earliest days of web application development, users' computers were very, very slow. Remember Netscape Navigator? The only way to develop productive web applications was to build large applications that ran on very large servers. Early applications like Amazon had to invest in hardware much faster than desktop PCs. Since just loading web pages at all put a strain on PCs, the hard work had to be done on the server side.

As we have seen Moore's law taking effect, we've seen users' computers getting faster and faster. Now even a smartphone has more processing power than the fastest desktops of the '90s. This is what has driven the new type of development that we've been discussing. Modern computers and smartphones are immensely faster and more capable than the computers in the early days of the Web; this is driving the migration to client-side composition and thick client-side logic.

Frameworks like SproutCore and Cappuccino would have been completely untenable in the days of Internet Explorer 3. Today, the hardware capabilities have increased to the point where client-side logic can run so quickly that it can create a better user experience for data to be composed in real time, like with Gmail and Twitter. It also provides a much easier, much more scalable system for modern application developers on the backend.

Monolithic web application development wasn't the best practice. It was simply the most practical method that you could take advantage of in the earliest days of the Web. Now we have progressed to the point where client-side computing is fast enough to enable the development of far more capable applications than we've ever seen before.

The best practices that we've discussed in this chapter have evolved based on the increasing speeds of CPUs and are a reflection of the effects of Moore's law. It is not a fashion statement, and it's transforming the way generations of developers are getting their jobs done.

CHAPTER 6

Mobile Apps on PaaS

The growth of mobile apps has pushed forward the model of creating services that are consumed through APIs to such a degree that APIs are now at the forefront of development. It has become a necessity, not a nice-to-have, to be able to create APIs and serve them at large scales.

Before we look at code examples for creating mobile apps on PaaS, let's put these new techniques in perspective by briefly examining their evolution.

A Brief History of Mobile App Development

Before the iPhone first hit the marketplace in 2007, mobile phones had an incredibly tightly controlled environment. It was difficult and often impossible to create third-party mobile applications, and there were strict limitations on what those applications could do. Even the mobile web had its own proprietary formats on early phones. They had their own versions of HTML, like TTML (Tagged Text Markup Language), WML (Wireless Markup Language), and HDML (Handheld Device Markup Language), that were stripped down to the bare minimum and included odd new, arbitrary tags so that they would work on these highly constrained devices.

The iPhone was the first cell phone to ever ship with a fully compatible HTML web browser.

On the original iPhone, third-party apps were originally built as HTML websites optimized for the phone's screen. Obviously, these were not yet native mobile applications; they were still browser based.

One of the early innovations in mobile application development was writing applications in straight HTML and CSS for phones. This was when we saw a shift in the way that mobile applications were created. At this point, creating a mobile application was still like creating a web application. You still had heavy server-side logic that would create and present all the information, with very little logic residing on the client side.

However, as the iPhone matured, and as Android and Windows Phone devices came to market with native mobile applications, the situation changed dramatically and quickly. Instead of generating HTML and CSS, you created APIs that would be fed into the native mobile client to be processed directly on the phone itself.

The native client might be running on iOS or Android, in an Objective-C or Java environment. These would usually be much heavier in client-side logic, with a lot of the presentation logic and all of the components for the user experience on the client side. Your backend systems therefore had to act and think differently. There would be APIs that fed into these client systems and were consumed by them. This mirrored much of what modern web development was moving toward: thicker client-side logic. On the Web, that meant a lot more JavaScript; in the mobile realm, it meant Objective-C or Java.

In any case, whether the client is a thick web client using JavaScript that consumes APIs or an Objective-C native mobile client, in the end you are going to need data to populate it with. Serving that data is still going to be a problem, no matter what kind of client consumes it. This situation pushed forward a resources-oriented method of creating lightweight JSON and XML services and metaservices to support these mobile applications.

The Apps of the Future

Looking forward, mobile applications will be gaining more and more functionality and speed. Even though modern smartphones are light-years more powerful than even a large computer was 10 years ago, they still have limited capacity and limited bandwidth compared to many desktop computers today. We can expect that phones are going to continue to get faster, cheaper, and smaller with much more functionality, driving even more client-side technology.

Then there's another important growth factor to consider: we have barely touched the surface of the penetration of the mobile marketplace. Estimates indicate that as of 2012, around 300 to 600 million smartphones were in use. But the ultimate market size of the smartphone era is estimated to be closer to 3 billion smartphones. In 2012, there were only 10% to 15% of the smartphones that will exist in 2022.

So, not only are we going to see apps with enhanced capabilities, but we are going to see a large increase in the number of people consuming these applications.

There is another trend worth noting: the bifurcation of popularity between iOS and Android, and the further splitting of the marketplace by enthusiasts of Windows smartphones and BlackBerry devices. Each of these platforms supports unique ways to build applications. As the smartphone market matures, the differences in technologies are going to become less and less tenable. Developers are going to come up with more creative ways to pack in the functionality, and do so in a way that can be consumed across many platforms at once, taking advantage of the whole mobile market.

Ultimately, there will be an increasing number of people consuming more services, creating higher loads for the backend applications that serve them. So we'll see the need for backend services and metaservices that are able to move to large scales and do so quickly. They will need to perform well while they gain popularity.

The key takeaway: developers need to think in terms of what it will take to get the backend services for these applications to run well at scale. And that is where PaaS is going to shine.

Data Structures

API-driven development models involve the use of data structures that serialize information into packets that can be distributed between devices. In this section, we'll review two of them: JSON and XML.

JSON and XML

A familiar activity involves taking a structure that has a username and a password, plus a list of friends encapsulating this data; you want to be able to send this data from a server to a client to be consumed by the end user. There are many ways to accomplish tasks like this.

XML is one common method that is prevalent within Java; it's still a vital tool within many enterprise applications. JSON is a bit newer to the market; it's a JavaScript representation of objects. JSON's relationship to JavaScript is key in understanding why this format has taken off.

One of the most common ways that JSON is consumed is through a JavaScript client on the web frontend. Because of that attribute, it is very easy to turn JSON into JavaScript objects through the web client. Since the point of origin of many mobile applications is the Web, these JavaScript representations have transferred with them. They are much easier for humans to read and much less verbose. They also take up less data, another reason these types of objects have proliferated within mobile devices.

XML is very verbose, which can be good when dealing with complicated data. However, it will add significant bulk to your data packets, and in mobile development, where you have limited bandwidth and you have to deal with slow connections, transferring as little data as possible becomes ever more important. This is why many mobile applications have chosen JSON for encoding and transferring data.

For reference, JSON has the following basic data types available:

- String
- Number
- Boolean
- Null
- Hash
- Array

Consuming Metaservices in Mobile Clients

Many mobile applications need data from the Internet in order to function. If you can build RESTful backend services like the ones mentioned in Chapter 5 and scale them in a PaaS environment, they can be consumed easily and quickly by mobile applications in any environment.

iOS

Native iOS applications in Objective-C can get data quickly and easily from metaservices. There are various ways you can approach this process, from building it yourself to leveraging open source or proprietary frameworks to help you.

The first step to writing the code yourself is leveraging iOS's asynchronous network operations:

1. Create an NSMutableURLRequest object that will represent the URL string.
2. Create an NSURLConnection object that will load the URL and return the data.
3. Create an NSMutableData object to store the response once it is received.

Here is an example of what that Objective-C code might look like in practice:

```
- (void)load {
  NSURL *myURL = [NSURL
    URLWithString:@"http://example.com/users"];
  NSMutableURLRequest *request = [NSMutableURLRequest
    requestWithURL:myURL
      cachePolicy:NSURLRequestReloadIgnoringLocalCacheData
    timeoutInterval:120];
  [[NSURLConnection alloc] initWithRequest:request
                                  delegate:self];
}

- (void)connection:(NSURLConnection *)connection didReceiveData:(NSData *)data {
    [mutableData appendData:data];
}
```

```
- (void)connection:(NSURLConnection *)connection
  didReceiveResponse:(NSURLResponse *)response {
    mutableData = [[NSMutableData alloc] init];
}

- (void)connection:(NSURLConnection *)connection
  didFailWithError:(NSError *)error {
    [mutableData release];
    [connection release];
    NSLog(@"Unable to fetch data");
}

- (void)connectionDidFinishLoading:
                    (NSURLConnection *)connection
{
    NSLog(@"Succeeded! Received %d bytes of data",
                            [mutableData length]);
    NSString *jsonResponse = [[[NSString alloc]
                    initWithData: mutableData
                        encoding: NSASCIIStringEncoding]
                    autorelease];
    // Parse the jsonResponse and feed it to the UI
}
```

As of iOS 5, Apple added native parsing of JSON through the NSJSONSerialization class; however, there are some open source libraries that can parse JSON even faster in iOS, like JSONKit (*https://github.com/johnezang/JSONKit*).

Once the data is grabbed and parsed, there are a number of ways to serve that data to the frontend user experience:

- Delegate the controller to the view that now has the data. This is straightforward to implement the view delegation methods, but it does not persist the data on the device.
- Persist the data on the device in a plist or archived format.
- Persist the data on the device using Apple's Core Data framework.

Apple's Core Data framework is Apple's standard way for iOS apps to persist data on phones. It is used widely for filling the UI components quickly and easily through many parts of the iOS experience.

iOS framework for REST: RestKit

RestKit (*http://restkit.org/*) is a popular open source framework for iOS that does a lot of the work described above automatically. It will handle the network-grabbing pieces and the JSON parsing, automatically populate the data into Core Data, seed the Core Data objects when you submit them to the App Store, provide an object mapping system, and more. Here is some example code that illustrates how easy it is to integrate example

RESTful URL *http://example.com/users* for adding a user's concept to your iOS application:

```
// User.h
@interface User : NSObject
@property (strong, nonatomic) NSString *name;
@end

// User.m
@implementation User
@synthesize name;
@end

// MasterViewController.m

#import <RestKit/RestKit.h>
#import "User.h"

...

- (void)viewDidLoad
{
    [super viewDidLoad];

    RKURL *baseURL = [RKURL URLWithBaseURLString:@"http://example.com/users"];
    RKObjectManager *objectManager = [RKObjectManager
    objectManagerWithBaseURL:baseURL];
    objectManager.client.baseURL = baseURL;

    RKObjectMapping *userMapping = [RKObjectMapping mappingForClass:[User class]];
    [userMapping mapKeyPathsToAttributes:@"name", @"name", nil];
    [objectManager.mappingProvider setMapping:venueMapping
    forKeyPath:@"response.users"];

    [self sendRequest];
}
```

It is obvious how much easier it is to use a library like this, but you do lose the ability to control a lot of the internal details if you need them.

Android

Android native applications use Java and can also get data quickly and easily from metaservices. As with iOS, there are various ways you can approach this process, from building it yourself to leveraging open source or proprietary frameworks to help you.

The first step to writing the code yourself is leveraging Android's asynchronous network operations:

1. Extend the `AsyncTask` class to make this an asynchronous task.

---

2. Create a `URLConnection` and convert the data into a string.

3. Process the results into a Java object.

Here is an example of what that Java code might look like in practice:

```java
// executed in a Service via new GetRESTData().execute();
// http://developer.android.com/reference/android/app/Service.html
private class GetRESTData extends AsyncTask <Void, Void, String> {

    @Override
    protected String doInBackground(Void... params) {
      URL url = new URL("http://example.com/users");

      URLConnection urlConnection = url.openConnection();
      InputStream in = new
        BufferedInputStream(urlConnection.getInputStream());
      BufferedReader reader = new
        BufferedReader(new InputStreamReader(in));
      String result, line = reader.readLine();
      result = line;
      while((line = reader.readLine())!=null){
          result += line;
      }
      in.close();

      return result;
    }

    protected void onPostExecute(String restResult) {
      // process the JSON string into a Java object
      // and persist it into a SQLite database
    }
}
```

Note that you should not implement Android REST methods inside activities. Activities are for user interface and user experience functionality. The code should always start long-running operations from a service; Android services were meant to run this kind of code.

Android has a native parser for JSON through the `org.json.JSONObject` class; there are also some open source libraries that can parse JSON in Android, like JSONLib (*http://json-lib.sourceforge.net/*), FlexJSON (*http://flexjson.sourceforge.net/*), and Gson (*http://code.google.com/p/google-gson/*).

Once the data is grabbed and parsed, it needs to be persisted immediately. SQLite is your best friend in Android. You should also use a sync adapter to execute regular checks for new data from your REST services. The sync adapter can change your data-grabbing process from a pull into a push architecture, which will save a ton of battery life.

Android framework for REST: Restlet

Like RestKit for iOS, there are REST libraries for Android. In fact, because Android uses Java, you can use the same REST client libraries in your Android native mobile apps as you do your Java web apps. Restlet (*http://www.restlet.org/*) is one such popular library that can save you time and headaches when getting data from RESTful resources.

 There are some good tutorials and books about Restlet; check out the website (*http://bit.ly/13TmPe6*) and *Restlet in Action* (*http://www.manning.com/louvel/*) by Jerome Louvel, Thierry Templier, and Thierry Boileau.

Here is what a simple Restlet implementation might look like:

```
public interface UserResource {
    @Get
    public User retrieve();

    @Put
    public void store(User user);

    @Delete
    public void remove();
}

ClientResource cr = new ClientResource("http://example.com/users/123");
// Get the User object
UserResource resource = cr.wrap(UserResource.class);
User user = resource.retrieve();
```

Restlet manages the JSON parsing and many other aspects, but your User class will still need to handle persistence to a SQLite database. For more information about this, take a look at *Android Cookbook* by Ian F. Darwin (specifically Chapter 11, which handles persisting data and parsing JSON in more detail).

How PaaS Makes Mobile Backend Development Easier

In this chapter, we have seen how easy it is to incorporate dynamic data into mobile applications when there are RESTful metaservices behind the scenes. There are many benefits PaaS brings when you build mobile applications this way. The following sections examine a few of these benefits.

It's Fast to Build Mobile Backend Metaservices

As seen in Chapter 5, building metaservices, which can power mobile or web frontends, is easy to do in Platform-as-a-Service. In fact, building applications in PaaS this way from the beginning is actually a best practice. These services have less code, are easier to maintain, and are easier to scale.

When you use a PaaS to build metaservices, deploying large N-tier clustered servers and managing them takes seconds, not weeks or months.

PaaS makes building and running metaservices faster and easier than ever before.

It's Easy to Scale Metaservices with PaaS

Scaling metaservices in PaaS is easy. If your app is modular and does not require constant disk access, you can very quickly and easily add more instances, which increases the concurrency levels dramatically. As thousands (or hopefully millions) of people start using your mobile applications, adding capacity is no longer a chore but an API call.

Many PaaS providers even have REST APIs, which you can use to automate the process of scaling.

It's Easy to Pick the Right Underlying Core Services

You might only have 1,000 users, but those users might upload 100,000,000 pictures. Your PaaS provider can make it easy to manage and run the proper scalable backend service to handle both kinds of services fast and effectively.

Portable Interfaces Can Be Used on Many Devices

Once you build your metaservices and launch them on a PaaS, they can be accessed through your iOS, Android, or Windows Phone smartphones and tablets. They can even power your web presence. This is a powerful way to maximize the efficiency of the resources you have when building applications.

Serving a Large Audience

To date, we have seen the growth of many different kinds of applications. In some cases, developers have created them in their basements and then leveraged PaaS, or tried to leverage one of the methods that we discussed earlier in this book, such as dedicated hosting. With a bit of luck, they might get featured on one of the app stores. And, as we've seen, the ensuing pressure on computing resources can sometimes ruin the developer's business.

The anticipated proliferation of mobile devices is going to exacerbate these kinds of problems for those who do not adopt PaaS to help them scale their applications. The audience for mobile apps is going to expand drastically, and that is going to make it even more difficult to create scalable backend infrastructures for anything but the simplest of phone applications.

CHAPTER 7

A Look at Core Services

When selecting a PaaS provider, it is important to understand what exactly you are getting yourself into. This chapter will focus on core services, not just the running of an application. When we talk about core services, we're talking about functions that provide data storage, SQL, NoSQL, queuing, and other support for applications. These core services can also include email monitoring, caching and data management, consumption and analysis, each of which can be an entire application of its own.

Typically a PaaS provider will manage the core services itself, or through a third-party add-on system that integrates tightly with the PaaS. Either way, when using PaaS you do not end up managing many of the core services yourself. This can clearly be beneficial (what developer really wants to spend her time tuning *my.cnf* files?), but it has some significant trade-offs as well, which we will explore in this chapter.

The goal for this chapter is to help you know what to expect from PaaS-based core services and what questions to ask potential PaaS providers before you commit to running production code on their systems.

Non-PaaS Core Services

PaaS is, by its nature, a very managed environment. You do not have to worry about scaling. You do not have to worry about the operations behind your application. You just know that you need to have it scale up or scale out; the major decisions are whether the app needs more RAM capacity or more instances. That will come to be what you expect out of your core services like MySQL and MongoDB as well. In fact, much of the time, core services can end up being just as difficult to run, scale, and manage as your applications, if not more so. That's because, if you are managing core services on your own, every service that you add can also add a huge amount of operational complexity.

When you consider hosting and managing a MySQL service, also consider how much time you'll spend managing it, monitoring it, and dealing with outages. Once you've worked with enormous data stores and terabytes of data, it becomes very clear that it's just as technically challenging to work with services like MySQL, PostgreSQL, MongoDB, and memcached in a distributed fashion as it is to work with your application code directly.

In a non-PaaS environment, you would have to set up MySQL. Then you'd have to tune it. You would have to set up your RAID disk backend for redundancy. Then you would have to devise external backup plans. You would have to set up master-slave replication, or sometimes even master-master replication with slaves. Then you would have to add heartbeat monitors to ensure that the system is continuously watching for outages and can deal with them. You have to be tuning, monitoring, and maintaining these core services all the time. You have to look for all sorts of very low-level network settings and make sure that you are constantly maintaining, managing, and dealing with security patches and upgrades.

Evaluating PaaS for Services

In a PaaS environment, a large chunk of these maintenance tasks are done for you automatically. Obviously, the quality of the operational excellence can range tremendously depending on what PaaS vendor you choose. So, evaluating the core services provided by each PaaS provider can at times be just as important as evaluating any other feature.

The end of this chapter has a checklist of questions you should have good answers to before committing to any vendor. It is critical you take these into consideration early in the decision-making process.

Look for what kinds of limitations you will run into:

- How much data storage is allowed?
- How much disk I/O is permitted?
- What happens when I hit my limits?
- How much RAM is available per service?
- How can I get more resources for my services if I need to scale?

When considering a PaaS provider, having this information ahead of time is important as it tells you whether or not you are going to be able to scale your application.

Keep in mind that with many applications you are never going to hit data barriers. Most applications do not need terabytes of disk. Most don't even need gigabytes. Generally, most applications need just tens of megabytes, with room to grow into the hundreds of megabytes.

So, you should be looking for and predicting how much data you are going to need to store in MongoDB, PostgreSQL, CouchDB, Redis, or memcached. You're trying to understand, "Does my PaaS allow me to grow? Or will it limit me and make it hard for me to move off?" You'll need to put in a little work up front talking and thinking about what your application is going to require at the higher end.

Some PaaS providers are going to be a lot better at this than others. But much of the time a PaaS platform will have already tuned the database, the configuration files, and the network interfaces so that they are significantly better than out of the box. It will have done a lot of thinking about failover and redundancy, which can be difficult problems to solve, especially if you are just a developer. Even operations teams can easily spend weeks or months planning and building out the procedures to do things that come right out of the box in a PaaS-managed service.

The benefits of using a PaaS for core services can be significant. You get up to speed much faster. You get to prototype faster. You get to write more code sooner. You don't have to worry about how to do a distributed memcached or master-master MySQL. You don't have to figure out how to get through SMTP filters for mail servers and through the spam filters at Google and Hotmail for sending email. PaaS can take much of the burden off your shoulders. A PaaS provider, giving you greater flexibility and speed, can do all of these things for you.

Saving Time with Managed Databases and PaaS

When you are trying to set up managed services on your own, the ones that can provide the biggest headaches are databases. Managing them and backing them up can take more time than writing the code for your application in the first place. The advantages of working with managed SQL core services in PaaS can be significant if you do your homework and make the right choices.

SQL

Working with SQL and PaaS can save an impressive amount of time. By relying on expertise that hopefully has been invested in creating a scalable SQL solution for you, you'll be able to work faster. But once again, there are several caveats.

You may need to consider the limitations on how many queries you're allowed. There are many different ways to charge for SQL core services:

- Number of queries you make to your database in a month
- Data storage capacity

- Number of concurrent users accessing data
- Some combination of these

These are very different ways to price the service and can lead to drastically different bills depending on your specific use cases.

Your decision will be highly dependent on several factors, given the type of application you are going to build. There are a few things that can change the dynamics when choosing a managed PaaS core service or going on your own.

Within the next 12 months, which of these answers will most likely be true in your case?

1. How much of the data can theoretically be cached most of the time?
   a. More than 50%
   b. Between 10–50%
   c. Less than 10%
2. How much is your app dynamic data driven, versus static content or objects storable?
   a. Less than 40% dynamic
   b. Between 40–60% dynamic
   c. More than 60% dynamic
3. How much data is stored in your database?
   a. Less than 5 GB
   b. Between 5 GB and 50 GB
   c. More than 50 GB
4. How many records need to be stored in any given table?
   a. Less than 10,000,000
   b. Between 10,000,000 and 100,000,000
   c. More than 100,000,000
5. How many tables do you need?
   a. Less than 20
   b. Between 20–100
   c. More than 100
6. How frequently will the data be accessed?
   a. Less than 10 times a second
   b. Between 10 and 100 times a second

c. Over 100 times a second

7. How much data needs to be accessed frequently and repeatedly?

    a. Less than 1 GB

    b. Between 1 GB and 10 GB

    c. More than 10 GB

If you answered (a) to 5–7 of these questions and (b) for the rest, you are a perfect candidate for most PaaS-managed core SQL services.

If you answered (b) to 3–7 of these questions, you will need to evaluate your PaaS options carefully and do load testing before committing to the PaaS vendor you select.

If you answered (c) to 2–3 of these questions, your best bet is to either run the core SQL service yourself if you are capable of doing so or select a provider that specializes in scaling the SQL service to the levels you need. You can still use PaaS for your application logic, but it is not a good idea to use it for your managed core data service if you are likely to hit these general guidelines.

Some applications will fit the mold and some will not. For example, consider a Word-Press database. This can be a highly cacheable application, so you end up not hitting the database with every query. It can be cached within the PaaS application environment easily. It can be highly optimized and relatively inexpensive to run, and doesn't usually require a lot of data to be stored.

However, when you have a PaaS provider that limits your concurrence on the database, it can be problematic if your blog or website is going to be handling a heavy load. Typically, blogs do not need to handle more than 10 requests a second—even that would be a generous amount of traffic. But there are times when you are going to want to ensure that you can deal with 1,000 requests a second. If your database is designed so that it can only do 10 concurrent requests, that is going to limit the ability to serve 1,000 people. Lots of those people are going to see error pages. The conclusion: knowing those limitations up front is important.

On the other hand, if you are being charged on a per-query basis and there is no limit to concurrence, you need to make sure that you optimize your code to minimize queries, which can get very expensive.

So, while you must keep close track of how you are being charged for your database, the potential benefits—the ability to save time and move quickly—are significant.

NoSQL

NoSQL is a type of key/value or document store database that is gaining popularity and has many forms, including MongoDB, CouchDB, Redis, Cassandra, and Riak. These technologies assist in scaling out in different ways than traditional SQL storage mechanisms.

The advantages of working with NoSQL and PaaS are similar to the ones you experience when working with SQL and PaaS, such as the ability to get started very quickly. You do not need to think about tasks like running your MongoDB service, managing it, or tuning it.

One of the benefits of self-managing NoSQL is that scaling out can be much easier compared to managing a MySQL, PostgreSQL, or traditional SQL database: you just add more virtual machines and tie those into the configuration. Not every PaaS provider allows you to grow quite as easily. It's a good idea to understand your contingency plan in the event that you need to scale bigger than the NoSQL capacity allowed within your PaaS.

Within the next 12 months, which of these answers is most likely to be true?

1. How much data is stored in your database?
   a. Less than 5 GB
   b. Between 5 GB and 50 GB
   c. More than 50 GB
2. How many records or documents need to be stored in any given table?
   a. Less than 100,000,000
   b. Between 100,000,000 and 1,000,000,000
   c. More than 1,000,000,000
3. How frequently will the data be accessed?
   a. Less than 10 times a second
   b. Between 10 and 100 times a second
   c. Over 100 times a second
4. How much data needs to be accessed frequently and repeatedly?
   a. Less than 1 GB
   b. Between 1 GB and 10 GB
   c. More than 10 GB

If you answered (a) to 3–4 of these questions and (b) for the rest, you are a perfect candidate for most PaaS-managed core SQL services.

If you answered (b) to 2–4 of these questions, you will need to evaluate your PaaS options carefully and do load testing before committing to the PaaS vendor you select.

If you answered (c) to 2–4 of these questions, your best bet is to either run the core NoSQL service yourself if you are capable of doing so or select a provider that specializes in scaling the NoSQL service to the levels you need. You can still use PaaS for your application logic, but it is not a good idea to use it for your managed core data service if you are likely to hit these general guidelines.

Caches and PaaS: Look for Redundancy

Typically, caches end up being stateless and volatile. There are a few popular caching technologies, some open source like memcached and Ehcache and some proprietary ones like TerraCotta for Java. They do not require as much overhead as a SQL or even a NoSQL database. It is easier to scale them and to run them. If they die it is not going to cause major problems, as long as there is redundancy in place.

The advantages of working with caches in PaaS actually outweigh some of the disadvantages of working with databases in PaaS, since often the hardest part of implementing caches is setting up redundancy, which is typically handled for you within a PaaS environment. Again, checking with your PaaS provider to ensure that there are redundancy and failover mechanisms in place is an important bit of research that needs to be done.

The only other consideration is the limit on how much data is cached. Sometimes a PaaS provider limits you to only being able to cache a certain amount of data. Often that will be sufficient, since most caching systems will purge the oldest (least recently used) data automatically, ending up with only the most important data in memory. However, if your dataset grows past the limit and you are constantly hitting your SQL or NoSQL backends, and your PaaS provider can't give you a higher limit, it's time to move to hosting the cache yourself.

Moving from a PaaS hosted cache to a self-managed caching system is not usually a very hard process since caches by nature are volatile, so it is not so important to set up a managed cache for yourself before you hit your limits.

Solving the Challenges of Email

Sending email in a cloud environment can be a very difficult proposition. When you are using virtual machines in Amazon Web Services, Rackspace, or Azure, they often have IP addresses that have been blocked by email providers. Big email providers like AOL and Gmail will block large groups of IP addresses owned by public cloud providers because spammers have regularly taken advantage of them in the past.

When using the public cloud, it is very likely that your application is going to run on an IP address that has been blacklisted by email providers, which leads to a question: how do you send email to your users within a PaaS public cloud environment? Also important for some applications is this associated question: how do you accept and process inbound email in your application?

If you are running a blog, this may not matter. But if you are running an interactive service and part of the service has to do with processing email, you'll be facing a unique set of challenges when using the public cloud.

The smartest approach is to leverage a managed email service. Often this service is going to be different than your database or caching service. It is likely not to be natively hosted with your PaaS provider. It is usually an independently run software service, and generally it will charge by how many emails you need to send. Sometimes your PaaS provider can facilitate the connection between your application and the email service by setting up an account for you. These kinds of services will send email for you, either one-off or in bulk. A key advantage is that the emails sent from these accounts have already been whitelisted by Gmail, AOL, and Hotmail, which means they are much more likely to get to your users' inboxes instead of being blocked by spam filters than if you sent them directly yourself.

You may not realize it, but being whitelisted and remaining whitelisted is actually a full-time job of its own. It is very difficult to keep up to date with the requirements that Google, AOL, Microsoft, and Yahoo! impose. Making sure that most users keep receiving communications is easy to do when you are only sending a few dozen emails a day, but it becomes incredibly difficult when you are sending hundreds or thousands a day. In the end, it just makes sense to leverage these services. You can go through third parties, but they may also be managed by your PaaS provider or by your IaaS provider.

Here is a list of a few popular mail services:

- Sendgrid (*http://sendgrid.com/*)
- Rackspace's Mailgun (*http://www.mailgun.com/*) (send and receive email)
- Amazon's Simple Email Service (*http://aws.amazon.com/ses/*)
- MailChimp (*http://mailchimp.com/*)
- Campaign Monitor (*http://www.campaignmonitor.com/*)

The Importance of Monitoring

Whether you are running your own infrastructure or building on PaaS, there is one challenge that is the same: monitoring all the pieces of your application.

This means knowing how much load your application has (right now and historically), and how your database is doing (in terms of transactions, disk I/O, memory, etc.). It also means understanding how many people are getting data concurrently (or trying to) and whether your service is succeeding or failing to serve them.

Considering Your Options

Monitoring options in PaaS can vary greatly. Some PaaS providers give you deep insight and have monitoring built in, others require third-party integrations, and yet others provide little to no insight.

Like your email service, monitoring can be provided either by a third party or natively by your PaaS platform. Many times it is a combination of both. There will be a set amount of information that your PaaS platform will give you about your application; the monitoring will show you some statistics, give you some baseline information, and perhaps integrate with third-party monitoring services to give you deeper information. For example, New Relic and AppFirst, which are third-party SaaS services, will give you very detailed information about how well your application is performing and when there are errors, and can even notify you if the application is not working or hits certain limits. These services can sometimes tell you how long it takes for your application to respond to a user and give you averages and historical information.

Monitoring is important for another reason. Traditionally, PaaS has been extremely easy to scale horizontally and sometimes even vertically. The hardest part is knowing when to scale. The vast majority of PaaS services do not have an auto-scaling feature that decides to add capacity to your application for you. But if you have a proactive monitoring service that informs you when you are hitting some limits, or when your application is running slowly, you can take action.

With information from monitoring services, you can set thresholds and even make your own auto-scaling functionality within the PaaS environment. Alternatively, you can simply go into the console and move the slider up and say, "I need more resources right now."

In any case, detailed information about monitoring is critical and should never be overlooked when running applications in PaaS. Much of the attraction of PaaS is that you don't have to worry about the operations behind your application or about tuning and configuring a lot of settings. But ultimately you need to be accountable and know how well your application is performing. Monitoring is essential for doing that. It should never be skipped, and it should be included in every application you run in a PaaS environment.

Here is a list of a few popular monitoring services:

- New Relic (*http://newrelic.com/*)
- AppFirst (*http://www.appfirst.com/*)
- AppDynamics (*www.appdynamics.com*)

Taking the Long View

Services are the spice of life in applications. They can turn simple applications into interesting ones. They can add value and depth to your application, but every time you add a new service it adds a layer of complication to the running and managing of your application, along with a set of limitations that you should always be aware of.

There are certainly large benefits to services. Every time you are evaluating whether you should build it or run it yourself, you should always think about seeing if a managed service is a better solution for you, because a managed service will likely save you a lot of time and money. But every time you pick a managed service, be aware that it is probably going to be priced in various ways, even if it is the same type of service offered by different providers.

Know how your application works. Use that knowledge to think months or years ahead and evaluate whether a managed service will still be a good fit down the road. This is an exercise that should always be performed.

The responsibility of using managed services comes with a price. The price is paid by planning ahead.

Load Testing

One of the most important parts of dealing with managed services is understanding the limitations of scale. To find those limits, you need to do performance tracking and load testing.

In many PaaS environments, there are add-ons and sometimes even native services that will do this for you. These services can test everything that we've discussed in this chapter —the monitor, database capacity, concurrence, limitations, and latencies—so that you can see how your application will perform when 1,000 people come to your site.

These kinds of services should be utilized after you've set up every other kind of managed service, then tied into your code. You can use them in different levels. You can see what it is like when 10, 10,000, or 100,000+ concurrent people are hitting your site so you can test your capacity planning. You can run fire drills to scale up both the instances of your application and also your database capacities to make sure that your team is ready to react proactively when your application is under siege.

Summing it up: performance and load-testing services are critical for working through many of the scaling use cases that we have been alluding to.

Here are a couple of popular load-testing services:

- Blitz (*http://blitz.io/*)
- Mu Dynamics (*http://www.mudynamics.com/*)

Planning an Upgrade Path

A final but very important consideration was touched on earlier in this chapter: you must plan ahead.

You need to think about how you can upgrade when you hit the limits. There are two clear choices:

- You can move within the PaaS to a higher limit.
- You can manage your own services.

How you proceed will depend on what PaaS you select, how it manages its systems, and how much access you get to those systems. There are PaaS providers that will let you upgrade seamlessly and allow you to up your resources, consumption, and concurrency with no change at all.

However, you should be aware that there are some providers that will require you to pick a new plan with a new data size, while they create a separate data storage container for you with higher limits. That new data storage will be bigger and have more capacity, but you are going to have to move your data and change your code. Sometimes the PaaS will do that for you, but that takes time. During the changeover, you are going to need downtime to migrate into the larger-capacity plan.

This process will be similar if you are going to move from a managed service to a non-managed one in which you do the management. If you need to create your own database to handle more capacity than the PaaS permits, you will have to set that up as a separate container and figure out a path similar to the one we just described in which you take your site down while you move the data over to the new database with the larger capacity.

Storage Options

In planning ahead for a PaaS upgrade, you should consider where your data is stored and how you are going to run the database yourself. For example, if your Platform-as-a-Service is hosted on Amazon Web Services in the US East data center, you might want to use virtual machines within that data center and manage MySQL yourself. You'll have to spin up the virtual machines within AWS, which will give you a low latency between the application and its data storage; in return you will get very high access, high speed, and high performance since they are colocated in the same network facility. It's difficult, but certainly achievable.

The same thing can be done in other hosting providers. You can find comparable solutions at Rackspace, HP Cloud, and Azure: if your PaaS runs in one of these infrastructures, you can spin up virtual machines within the same infrastructure and enjoy low-latency connections between your application and the data. You will not have to manage the application and the scaling of the application, but you will have to manage the database.

Alternatively, certain IaaS providers can manage your services. Sometimes they will offer even greater levels of control or different feature sets compared to PaaS providers. One example of this is Amazon's Relational Database Service (RDS). It has a great deal of functionality and can be used as its own managed service outside of any PaaS. So, if you choose one PaaS to run your application, you can choose Amazon RDS on the same infrastructure provider to achieve low latency. Your application can talk to that RDS database directly. If you ever choose to move your application to a different PaaS provider that is also on AWS, you can remain with that same RDS, which could be talking to a completely different PaaS provider. This gives you a little bit of flexibility in where you run your application.

In summary, it's important to think ahead and have plans on how to approach and get past the scalability limits of managing your data. As long as you have thought through these scenarios, it will be easy to get started with a managed service within the PaaS.

When considering a PaaS for managed services, it's essential to evaluate the provider's features and limitations. Here are some questions for you to ask when selecting a PaaS provider:

General questions
- How much data storage do apps have access to?
- Does the app expect persistent disk storage?
- Can applications write files to the disk?
- Are the files being written to the disk ephemeral?
- How much RAM is available to an application instance?
- What happens if my app hits that RAM limit?

Databases
- How will the provider charge?
- Queries per month?
- Data storage capacity?
- Number of concurrent connections?
- Is redundancy provided?

- Is there a failover mechanism in place?

Caches
- Is redundancy provided?
- Is there a failover mechanism in place?

Email
- Can the provider facilitate a connection between your app and an email service?
- Can the provider set up an email account for you?
- What third-party email service(s) does it work with?

Monitoring
- What kind of monitoring insight does the provider offer?
- What kind of control do you have?
- Does the provider have an auto-scaling feature?
- Will it notify you when you are hitting the limits?

Performance
- Does the provider offer performance statistics or have add-ons that have them?
- Does it provide load-testing services?

CHAPTER 8

Why Not PaaS?

Much of this book has focused on the benefits of PaaS and the compelling reasons why you might consider using a PaaS provider. But this chapter will take a look at the other side of the coin: in what situations might PaaS not be advantageous?

The answer depends on who you are and where you are coming from. If you are a developer within an enterprise, if you are working in a small- to medium-sized business, or if you are an independent developer or a hacker, the constraints are very different. In each of these cases, you'll be looking at Platform-as-a-Service through different lenses. And through those lenses, you'll also need to consider the pros and cons of the two very different ways to use PaaS: the public cloud PaaS and the private cloud PaaS.

Public Cloud versus Private Cloud

The public cloud usually runs on a public Infrastructure-as-a-Service platform (e.g., Amazon Web Services), and that's where you'll find PaaS providers like Heroku, EngineYard, and AppFog. In many PaaS options, you do not get to choose where exactly your code is run. You don't have much control over what is going on in the service, nor do you get to see the underpinnings of the operating system. You provide the code and the PaaS does the rest. The downside is that you do not get to have much insight into what is actually going on in the servers.

What Is Private Cloud?

In general, the term "private cloud" refers to a cloud computing platform that runs on hardware you control. Private cloud, however, is a controversial term. Some people even claim it does not exist, because they say it's not cloud if you are running it yourself. Others say that if you put IaaS or PaaS technology on servers you own or manage, that is sufficient to call it cloud.

For the purposes of this section, we will assume that private cloud means running IaaS or PaaS technology in an environment where you own or manage the servers.

Private cloud PaaS is less familiar to most developers than its public counterpart. When people think about PaaS, they generally think about public PaaS. It is the PaaS that most people are more comfortable with.

Private PaaS takes many different forms, but essentially it involves running PaaS on your own hardware, possibly directly on servers that you own. It can run on top of an on-premise IaaS platform, like OpenStack, vSphere, CloudStack, or Eucalyptus, or even directly on your unvirtualized hardware. The difference is that typically with private cloud PaaS you are the one running the PaaS code and you have to manage the code itself.

People running private cloud as opposed to public cloud PaaS get similar functionality and deployment mechanisms for the running of applications, but they are responsible for operating the PaaS code and making sure it stays running. This gives you added flexibility because you get more control over the servers; you can use your own servers and you do not have to be tied to a particular infrastructure provider.

There are some providers, like AppFog and OpenShift, that can actually run on both public and private clouds; these providers let you choose whether you want to host your applications on your existing dedicated infrastructure or on a public cloud. However, many of the other PaaS providers do not provide that choice.

How to Choose: Small- and Medium-Sized Businesses

If you are working for a small- or medium-sized business, the restrictions for where your code is run are generally somewhat flexible. You have some say in where you get to run your applications. Typically, privacy concerns are not as strong and security concerns about the public cloud are not as worrisome as they can be for big enterprise developers. This gives you more leverage in picking which one you feel is correct for your development. However, it is still a good idea to at least consider some options of flexibility. Make sure to check with your bosses to see if there are any strong opinions one way or another about public and private cloud in the future.

As an independent developer, you have all the choice in the world. Surprisingly, you still might want to think about private cloud options, especially if you are a tinkerer. Installing Cloud Foundry (PaaS) or OpenStack (IaaS) on your own systems is definitely very hard, but it can also be a lot of fun to figure out how they work.

Many independent developers often want things to just work and not to have to worry about maintenance; for most independent developers, a public cloud PaaS is the right choice. You don't have to worry about servers or networks dying and keeping up with operating system patches. On the other hand, as an independent tinkerer, you may be curious about how it all works, or want to have more control, or want to be able to change things slightly or drastically. A private cloud can give you that flexibility. Being able to look at the source code, make changes, then run those changes can be very empowering.

In that light, let's look at some options for private cloud PaaS.

Open and Closed

In the arena of private cloud PaaS, you can choose between open source and closed source options. Enterprises and independent hackers can evaluate both.

For example, Cloud Foundry is an open source project that can run many different technologies. It does not care where it runs or how it runs. In fact, you can run it on your laptop and get PaaS functionality. The downside is that running it in production is very, very hard. It is a large distributed program and scaling it is a very difficult problem. There are providers like AppFog and Tier 3 that will do this for you, but you can also do it yourself.

Another open source tool is OpenShift by Red Hat. It is also something you can tinker with and run yourself, but it has different architecture than Cloud Foundry. You can get managed versions from Red Hat. For the independent hacker, these two options are the leading open source ones.

Cloudify is another open source PaaS. This one is aimed more toward enterprises than independent developers, and GigaSpaces (creator of Cloudify) has commercial support for it. While it is more geared toward Java, it does have support for some other technologies. (Compare Cloudify to choices such as Cloud Foundry, which have strong support for many technologies: Java, Node, PHP, Ruby, Python, and many others.)

Apprenda is a closed source PaaS specifically built for .NET. It has the added benefit of some runtime .NET functionality that no other .NET PaaS provides.

Here are some resources for getting started:

- Cloud Foundry (*http://cloudfoundry.org/*)
- OpenShift (*https://openshift.redhat.com/*)
- Cloudify (*http://www.cloudifysource.org/*)
- Apprenda (*http://apprenda.com/*)

How to Choose: Enterprise Businesses

Many enterprises and large businesses have strict data restrictions; they cannot let data leave their data centers. So when an enterprise is evaluating Platform-as-a-Service options, the public cloud PaaS providers are usually nonstarters because they cannot connect to the data sources they need to. This precondition makes private cloud PaaS a more viable solution for most enterprises, so developers within large enterprises will have to convince their technical leaders to bring PaaS in house.

However, for some use cases within large businesses, the public cloud is being increasingly accepted as a viable option—e.g., for running applications that aren't operationally critical and data sensitive. The three areas where the most public cloud adoption is happening within enterprises are mobile, social, and consumer web applications. These kinds of applications tend to be able to work without as much sensitive data; therefore, in these instances public cloud options are more acceptable.

As a developer, it is incredibly important to be careful when considering your options. Before you commit to a PaaS provider, it is very important to know whether it has an on-premises, private cloud offering. If you start out with a public cloud PaaS that cannot go on-premises, you might end up being told that you need to use a completely different PaaS. That could make your development much harder and involve a lot of transitions because the enterprise might have picked a private cloud PaaS; they might force you, at some point, to move to that one. If you choose a PaaS that has both public and private cloud offerings, you will have more flexibility in case there is a time when you need to go onto a private cloud; the same interface that you originally wrote will continue to function.

The Limitations of PaaS

Platform-as-a-Service has many benefits. But since this chapter is about PaaS limitations and why it might *not* be right for you, let's get negative for a few pages.

As a developer, PaaS can make your life easier. It can help you run and scale applications with fewer worries and less overhead. But it has limitations and boundaries in functionality, both in terms of what you can do with your code and also in what kinds of applications are best run within PaaS.

The limitations look and feel different depending on where you are coming from, where you work, and what you are using it for. If you are just looking at it from a coding perspective, there are a number of drawbacks. A general lack of filesystem support means that you need to think ahead for scaling multiple instances of your site. Other limitations: sometimes you have to write code specific to the platform, which makes it less portable, and sometimes you get less insight into how it is running.

Many of these technical limitations may improve over time. As various generations of PaaS move forward, we might see some of these tactile limitations go away. However, there still are other limitations that are going to be harder to deal with.

Fitting Your App into the Mold

As a developer, you have to think hard about what kind of application you are trying to build and whether it fits into the PaaS model. High-frequency trading applications for the stock market are never going to be an ideal use case for Platform-as-a-Service. Super-high-performance situations in which every microsecond is critical may not be ideal for PaaS for a long time. PaaS really is intended to solve some hard problems, but in the process it only addresses applications that fit within some sort of standardized molding. The more you get fancy and try to add many different kinds of features and functionality to a single application, the less likely it is to fit into the PaaS model.

Here is one example in Node. Developers sometimes build Node applications that open two network ports at the same time, accepting data from each port independently, with both feeding into one single application. A typical standard for PaaS is to have only one port open to the Internet, and that doesn't fit the mold for this kind of application, so building apps like this does not typically work well within Platform-as-a-Service.

Monolithic applications that have a big filesystem, a lot of functionality, and use many gigabytes of RAM are also not ideal candidates to work within the limitations of PaaS. When it is hard to decompose applications into smaller components and services, it tends to be harder to justify running them within a PaaS. Trying to debug deep problems in complicated apps running in production, depending on which PaaS you are using, can be very difficult and frustrating. This process really lends itself best to local development environments so that you can dive into some of the runtime details that are not available within a production environment.

More Considerations

Another limitation involves building distributed applications on PaaS. With highly distributed applications, you have to be aware of the message bus and understand whether your PaaS allows the message bus technology you depend on to connect your distributed applications. Whether you are using a message queue system or a database system in your distributed application, making sure that the pieces that you need to glue together are all well supported within a PaaS environment is another consideration.

Other limitations might be institutional. If you are working within a small- to medium-sized business or an enterprise, there may be an operations team who is responsible for running your applications and you might not even have a choice. There are cases where you can do your own development on a PaaS and hand that app to the operations folks, and they will get it working without a PaaS. So sometimes you can do your development in a PaaS and not have to worry about how it is ultimately deployed. But other times this becomes a problem; the cultural boundaries of what your operations team allows you to do will prevent you from running applications in a PaaS environment. We'll take a further look into cultural considerations later in this chapter.

Also consider the services and databases that you are using. If you are building an application that is going to require master-master replication and high availability, and if your system is going to require many gigabytes of database storage, you should think about these factors up front and make sure that the PaaS you choose supports your requirements. If you can't trust that this will be the case, PaaS may not be for you at this time.

In general, you should always check with your bosses to make sure they know where you are running your applications; not getting the OK from above is another reason why you might not be allowed to use a Platform-as-a-Service. System administrators are the ones that get the phone calls at 4 a.m. if it all breaks, and they can sometimes be resistant to new tools and technologies, so checking with them is an important thing to do in any business.

If you are working in an enterprise or a government agency, the data restrictions can be very limiting, and that might prevent you from picking a PaaS. If you have to go with a private cloud PaaS, there might be limitations on what languages it supports and how well it supports them.

If you are dealing with high-performance tweaks, if you have to customize your version of Ruby, if you are changing the internals of your runtime (like PHP), some PaaS vendors may allow that flexibility, but some will not. If you need to custom-compile your own version of Python, PaaS might not be the right fit. If you need to use a certain kind of processor or a certain kind of hardware to run your application, it might not work with the PaaS you choose.

Ultimately, when you are weighing the limitations and benefits of PaaS, it is a matter of control. The more control you are willing and able to give up, the more PaaS functionality you will be able to leverage. So, the two sides of the scale are control and how much power you get from your PaaS. The degree to which you'll experience the advantages of velocity, speed, and time to market will depend on how much control you are willing to give up. Typically, the more you are able to fit into the mold of PaaS, the less you have to worry about the running of your application.

Avoiding Limitations

It is easy to shop around to find a PaaS that fits your needs. One of the strongest points about PaaS is how easy it is to set up and try out. You should evaluate the ease with which you get your first application running. This is a good indicator of not only the quality of the service, but also how you are going to be interacting with that service going forward.

As an informed developer, perform a survey:

1. Sign up for accounts on three different PaaS providers (most of them offer a free trial).
2. After some exploration of the options, dig deeper into the two you like most.
3. Deploy an application on both PaaS providers.
4. Play with their core services. How much data can you put into the database? Can the core services scale up?
5. Spend time delving into the service's functionality. Do you need a message bus? Do you need queuing or caching services?
6. Review the pricing structures.
7. Present the results to your superiors or operations team. If you are a solo developer, you should already know which one you want to use by now.

How to Determine the Cost of a PaaS

One of the downsides to Platform-as-a-Service is that while it is so simple to set up, there seem to be many different ways to price it. This can be extremely confusing, especially if you're new to PaaS. This becomes critical when you need to scale: how much will you pay? Let's examine this question, keeping in mind that this is a snapshot in time. It's important to note that over time, the pricing methods are likely going to change as well.

Here's a typical scenario with many PaaS providers.

You've launched your app. Soon you need to handle more traffic and your application needs to grow. How will this affect your bill? Many small businesses end up scaling into accounts that, in 2013, cost $2,000 to $3,000 a month in PaaS. When they reach those price points, many developers realize that they might be able to rent a much more powerful server for $300 a month. They drop Platform-as-a-Service and start managing their applications themselves. They give up all the benefits of PaaS because the bill has grown too quickly. Oftentimes, they overlook the opportunity to reevaluate the PaaS pricing options of other providers. With a quick survey of providers, you may find that for some reason or another, you can move from one PaaS at $3,000 a month to another PaaS at $300 a month.

Different PaaS providers have different ways to price. Some have pricing tiers, and others have more dynamic scale. With some providers (e.g., AppFog), you get a set amount of RAM for free and you can upgrade to higher tiers of RAM, which you can use in any way you want. Other providers are free in a sandbox mode, and only begin charging when you're in production. Heroku, for example, has a utilization-based dynamic fee scale in which you're charged for the resources you use in real time. If you use five additional apps for five minutes and then go back down to one, it'll charge you for the five minutes. Heroku charges per instance of your application instead of by the amount of RAM you use.

The key takeaway: try various PaaS providers before you subscribe, and be clear about what they're providing and for how much.

Encountering Resistance

Developers love PaaS. But sometimes others groups within a business are more resistant to adopting PaaS. The boss might not have heard of it and could be scared of it. A system administrator might feel like it would be out of his control; he might feel his job is threatened. Operations teams might feel like it goes around them. Even other developers might have resistance. They might feel like they know better or they have different ways that they've traditionally done things; they may have heard of PaaS and might not have a positive a reaction to it.

When you are interacting with these different groups, the facts that you've learned in this book can be used to explain and disarm many of their concerns. Being up-front about both the benefits and the limitations, showing that you understand these, and explaining why PaaS is acceptable for your application needs can be very powerful.

Explain that you'll be able to get your work done faster, that PaaS is more reliable and more scalable, and that you (and everyone else) won't need to worry as much at 4 a.m. Explain that when you need to move into a hundred different instances behind your application, you can do so with a click. These can be compelling arguments. When you're dealing with system administrators and operations people, be prepared to show that you understand the limitations of PaaS and its potential pitfalls (Table 8-1). Then explain how the PaaS provider you've chosen can help you manage the risk, and show them that you have plans to manage the limitations. Being prepared with these kinds of arguments can really disarm much of the resistance you may encounter within the operations and system administrator teams.

Table 8-1. Arguments for and against PaaS

PaaS benefits	PaaS limitations
The scalability of dedicated hosting	Large monolithic apps are problematic
The ease of shared hosting	Potential conflicts with data restrictions
Faster app development and deployment	General lack of filesystem support
N-tier is built in	Can't handle super-high-performance situations
Backend is fully managed	Customizing runtimes can be problematic
Less up-front expense than your own servers	More ongoing monthly expense than owning your own hardware

Use the empty spaces in Table 8-1 to fill in some of the benefits and limitations specific to your applications needs. Many trade-offs have been discussed in the earlier chapters.

Putting the Limitations in Perspective

As we finish our look at the limitations of PaaS, it's important to keep in mind that the next generations of PaaS are going to be more and more powerful. Platform-as-a-Service is just as important and disruptive a technology as virtualization was, and we are going to start seeing it becoming more and more standard. As it evolves, it's going to become just as important in enabling technology as virtualization is today. By the end of the 2010s, it will be the de facto way to run applications at scale.

We have not yet seen PaaS powering big applications like Facebook and Twitter. Certainly the limitations we've discussed in this chapter show why PaaS is not suited to these types of applications. It was built for lower levels of scale. It will help you get on your way to becoming a Facebook or a Twitter, but we haven't seen PaaS used at that large a scale before. While you won't see that happen today, PaaS will eventually arrive at the point where it will be powering the next mega-successful app.

The benefits of PaaS are going to continue increasing and the limitations are going to keep decreasing. And though there may be reasons today not to choose to run applications on PaaS, the forward thinkers that do end up running their applications on PaaS are the ones who are going to be getting their jobs done faster than their compatriots. They are the ones who are going to be getting promoted for making better choices and gaining recognition as forward thinkers—as the ones who are building for the future.

CHAPTER 9

The Future of PaaS

In the previous chapters, we began to look at what the future may hold for Platform-as-a-Service. PaaS will play an increasingly important role in app development as it matures through technological hurdles. Equally important to the future of PaaS, however, is the growth and influence of IaaS technology. The multitude of IaaS APIs can be confusing for a developer, but PaaS can offer a simpler worldview that lets developers get their work done faster.

The Influence of OpenStack

PaaS is often tied to Infrastructure-as-a-Service. The early PaaS companies, such as Heroku and EngineYard, used Amazon Web Services as their IaaS provider. As PaaS continued to evolve, an important technology shift occurred in IaaS. It all started from a simple question: what if Amazon Web Services technology was open source?

In July 2010, Rackspace and NASA jointly launched a new open source initiative known as OpenStack (*http://www.openstack.org/*). The idea was to create the world's first open source IaaS project. The first code contributions came from NASA's Nebula platform (called Nova) and Rackspace's Cloud Files platform (called Swift). The promise of OpenStack was enormous. If it could be built, theoretically anyone could run their own AWS-like service. Such a large promise turned out to be very hard to execute on. Early on, there were a lot of complaints about how immature the software was. However, it has matured quickly and is becoming more and more stable and feature rich every day.

OpenStack has become so successful in the few years since its inception that now there are at least two large public clouds that any developer can use based on it: one from Rackspace, and another from HP. IBM, Dell, and many others plan to utilize OpenStack in key product offerings in the future. There are literally hundreds of companies, large and small, that have committed time, money, and resources to making OpenStack a huge success.

OpenStack's success has been so great that other projects have sprung up like it. For example, CloudStack started out as a closed source system and is now open source as well, under the Apache 2.0 license; it is now managed by the Apache Foundation.

OpenStack's success has opened up possibilities for both the public cloud and the private cloud, providing more options on which PaaS can be built. Since a lot of PaaS technology depends on APIs for provisioning servers, and since OpenStack and CloudStack now provide options to do this in private clouds, PaaS is becoming more and more important in both public and private clouds.

Currently, the adoption of OpenStack is driving a new wave of IaaS options for companies like Rackspace. Rackspace started out as a managed hosting provider, offering managed services as well as managed servers. The company took a leadership position in OpenStack development because it wanted to offer OpenStack hosting on its managed platform, like Amazon Web Services, but with a technology that can be used in different ways. Rackspace accomplished that and now has a cloud system running on OpenStack; it's available in the public and private cloud.

Keeping Your Development Options Open

When you decide to choose an IaaS provider, you'll find that there are an abundance of options. But, while offering you the luxury of choice, this abundance of providers can be frustrating and confusing.

You can go with the incumbent Amazon Web Services or you can try out OpenStack or CloudStack, but be prepared to learn all the different APIs. You can also choose a proprietary system like Joyent or Azure, which have even more proprietary APIs. As you start building your applications, they will become more and more tied to the platforms you choose. The nature of IaaS is to lock you into one infrastructure provider; as you use it more, you become more dependent on it.

As a developer, you just want to get your job done. You want to get resources up and running. But creating new infrastructure on these different platforms becomes problematic given how complex and different their APIs end up being. Also, figuring out the different ways to consume IaaS on different infrastructures can be a very tedious task and not very much fun.

PaaS has the ability to actually run on different infrastructures and incorporate them in a way that doesn't have to look different. Your PaaS does not have to look different on OpenStack than it does on AWS, or on CloudStack. The version that is being run in a private cloud on-premises doesn't have to differ from the public-cloud versions. This gives PaaS more flexibility than IaaS. It can be run in different environments that have different APIs, so as a developer, you do not have to figure out the differences. This can be a big time-saver for developers when creating applications and trying different infrastructures to run those applications on.

Outages: Your Biggest Problem

Running infrastructure on different providers is incredibly difficult. Not only do you need to figure out the different APIs, but you also must figure out how to monitor and maintain your applications within those environments, which can be a Herculean task. To add to your headaches, you also have to deal with large-scale cloud outages.

It seems that every other week a big cloud provider goes down and takes half the Internet with it. This raises an incredibly important problem—perhaps the most important problem that application developers have had to deal with in the last decade.

How can you build a reliable and robust application on infrastructure that is not reliable and robust, and on data centers that are not reliable and robust?

A modern developer has to question whether keeping applications within a single provider is a good enough solution anymore. Whether you can trust a single IaaS provider or region becomes a difficult question to answer. If you cannot trust your infrastructure, the consequences of that are also difficult to manage. Here are some additional questions to consider:

- How do you manage failover, application redundancy, and high availability when applications are running simultaneously within two different vendors (e.g., AWS and Rackspace or HP and Azure)?
- How can you ensure that the code is running on the same systems and that the data can be accessible?
- How do you deal with a problem if one of those data centers goes down?
- How do you keep your website running during critical times?

These are very difficult questions, made even more difficult by the variety of available IaaS technologies. OpenStack can help resolve these problems by providing solutions in the public cloud and in the private cloud, but having the same IaaS technology in private and public clouds is only a partial solution. The way that infrastructure providers choose their technologies leads to variety; that variety makes high availability and failover harder to think about.

So, PaaS has a huge opportunity—the opportunity to be a technology that lives one layer higher in the stack. Platform-as-a-Service can think about and manage the IaaS for you. It can understand OpenStack APIs just as well as it can AWS APIs, and make them somewhat, if not fully, transparent to developers.

With PaaS, a developer doesn't have to realize that the underlying infrastructure is consumed, built, or managed in different ways; that gives PaaS a unique ability to provide insight at higher layer than the infrastructure level. It also makes it easier to think about failover and high availability than it is at the IaaS level. If you do indeed use OpenStack in the public and private clouds, there might be failover and high availability options for you that do not exist otherwise. However, configuring and managing two data centers without PaaS is still an incredibly huge headache.

We are living in a world where the ideal of having one technology everywhere is increasingly less likely to ever be realized. This means you may have to deal with a proprietary closed source system that is fundamentally different than what you are running internally. And this is why PaaS will prove so valuable. It can step in and fill that gap where IaaS can't.

Regaining Control Through Open Source

Open source PaaS options like Cloud Foundry, OpenShift, and Cloudify are using community leadership to build broad and deep operational knowledge into PaaS in a sustainable way.

Originally written by Derek Collison at VMware, Cloud Foundry is a set of more than a dozen programs that are loosely coupled and work together to provide PaaS functionality. Keep in mind that Cloud Foundry alone does not provide everything you might have come to expect from PaaS as described in this book. Cloud Foundry can be very difficult to set up and run at scale on your own. There are some providers that have done this hard work for you, like AppFog and CloudFoundry.com (*http://cloudfoun dry.com*), and there are ways you can set up Cloud Foundry in development mode easily on your laptop, but like OpenStack, it is only as powerful as the team operating it.

However, the Cloud Foundry library does provide many of the features you've come to expect with PaaS: being able to deploy apps with a command-line interface to a REST API, scaling and load balancing your application without configuring anything, and adding database and caching services like MySQL and Redis. Cloud Foundry can get these things up and running quickly and easily, but if it breaks, you need to be operationally knowledgeable about how to debug Cloud Foundry to find the problem. You also need to know how to run and scale MySQL as it grows.

One of the biggest concerns developers have about PaaS is giving up too much control and having to strictly conform to exactly how the PaaS vendor wants things to work. Open source libraries like Cloud Foundry and OpenShift are beginning to break down those concerns. Because they are fully open source, you can dig into their guts to see exactly how Apache and MySQL are configured. You can also create new runtime support—for example, the Erlang community has added Erlang support to Cloud Foundry.

In short, there's a lot of sophisticated technology behind open source PaaS technology, making it a powerful choice and a strong tool for developing the next generation of PaaS services.

Micro Magic

With these open source PaaS libraries, the first thing any developer wants to do is get a local copy running. You can do this in a few different ways.

Cloud Foundry offers a product called Micro Cloud Foundry that you can use to run your own local cloud. It runs on a Mac, a PC, even on Linux—basically anything that can run VMware Player, Workstation, or Fusion. Micro Cloud Foundry contains all of the independent services, so you can run all of Cloud Foundry on a single virtual machine.

However, it does not have the sophistication of a production-ready Cloud Foundry. For example, Cloud Foundry knows how to make adjustments—like, if you have five applications running on a single machine and that machine dies, as long as there is a slack pool of other virtual machines whose job it is to run applications, Cloud Foundry can redeploy applications automatically onto the available machines.

Vagrant is an open source library that lets you set up customized virtual machines locally, quickly and easily. Red Hat has detailed instructions on how to set up an OpenShift instance, but this can be tedious and difficult to do on your own. An alternative is to leverage technology like Vagrant to do this for you. Others have already done this and open sourced the result.

Setting up local bootstrapped copies of PaaS libraries like Cloudify is even easier; they were built as private only PaaS solutions, which means they were intended to be easy to set up. Cloudify has some great documentation about how to get started.

Here are some resources to guide you:

- Micro Cloud Foundry (*https://micro.cloudfoundry.com/*)
- Vagrant (*http://www.vagrantup.com/*)
- How to Set Up OpenShift (*https://openshift.redhat.com/community/wiki/build-your-own*)
- Vagrant File for OpenShift (*https://github.com/mojolingo/puppet-openshift*)
- Cloudify Setup Guide (*http://www.cloudifysource.org/guide/*)

Limitations of Open Source PaaS Libraries

PaaS libraries still need to be operated and maintained, and many open source PaaS libraries are limited in similar ways. As a developer, running a PaaS library can be hair-raising if you do not know what those limitations are.

One limitation is that a PaaS library usually can't launch more IaaS servers for you. Even if you have a slack pool of app servers waiting for new code to be deployed, if every one of the slack pool machines dies, Cloud Foundry doesn't know how to start more servers to add to the slack pool. It does not know how to operate the entire system and it doesn't know how to monitor and maintain itself. This can be an enormous chore for a small or even a large company trying to run Cloud Foundry.

Monitoring, managing, and maintaining the components of a PaaS library can be a big challenge. But the technology itself represents what the future of PaaS might look like; it can be run in ways that are very distributed, and it can operate in the public and private clouds, even on a laptop. It's important to understand that PaaS libraries deliver a high degree of flexibility, as long as you know how to harness that flexibility.

The Virtues of Versatility

One reason that PaaS is so well suited to open source projects is because it handles a significant challenge. If one company was especially good at PHP or Python or Perl, the task of building a PaaS for PHP or Python or Perl alone might be manageable. But the task of writing a PaaS that runs on Python, Perl, PHP, Java, .Net, Node, and every other technology you can think of is a difficult one. Being able to run many different technologies and being able to be very good at those technologies is a major asset of PaaS.

This versatility draws on a key strength of the open source movement. The ability to build on the work of open source collaborators and their contributions to the community is a significant reason why open source works so well with PaaS.

Final Thoughts

In the future, we're going to see more attempts at building a sustainable PaaS service that tries to tackle a significant problem: developers want to use PaaS, but it's very difficult right now for companies, both big and small, to adopt it. This has led to a dilemma in how to deliver PaaS. But over time we're going to see more and more companies trying to solve this problem so that developers can keep writing code the way they want to.

PaaS will to continue to be adopted by developers. They will start thinking about ways they can use PaaS more, and they'll start working around its limitations and using it in more creative ways. Platforms will start to adopt more use cases, be more flexible, and offer higher performance. But developers are truly reaping the benefits of PaaS right now. That is what's pushing PaaS forward as a development methodology—one that that's going to continue to flourish with the next generation of applications.

CHAPTER 10

Resources

Throughout this book, various tools and technologies have been mentioned. In this final chapter is a list of those resources, by category. Since PaaS and its related services are in a constant state of evolution, no fixed list of resources can truly be complete. But the following links will, at the very least, provide a starting point for your research.

PaaS Providers

PaaS providers come in many flavors. It can be hard to distinguish which one is right for your needs sometimes, but some of the biggest differences between PaaS vendors can be understood when you determine the languages their offerings support, the portability of apps in the PaaS, what infrastructure the PaaS runs on, and whether you are responsible for running the PaaS or the vendor does that for you. The following terminology is important to keep in mind:

Portable
> If you can easily move your application from one PaaS vendor to another, both are portable PaaS options. A PaaS that can run code largely unchanged from normal development processes is portable. For example, if the PaaS supports PHP and you can upload a WordPress PHP application without changing the fundamental code behind WordPress, this is a portable PaaS.

Non-portable
> A PaaS that is bound to proprietary APIs that make it difficult to move to other PaaS vendors is non-portable.

Public cloud
> Any PaaS that works on public clouds like AWS and Rackspace is a public cloud PaaS.

Private cloud

Any PaaS that works behind firewalls and on your own infrastructure is a private cloud PaaS.

Managed

A managed PaaS is a PaaS that you do not need to operate; you use it as a service.

Unmanaged

An unmanaged PaaS is a PaaS that needs to be set up, secured, maintained, operated, and updated manually.

Here is a list of current PaaS providers:

AppFog: portable, managed, public and private cloud

AppFog (*http://www.appfog.com/*)—now owned by CenturyLink (*http://www.centurylink.com/*)—was one of the first providers of first-class PHP support in PaaS. It has since grown in popularity and expanded to support Node.js, Ruby, Python, and Java solutions.

Apprenda: non-portable, unmanaged, public and private cloud

Apprenda (*http://www.apprenda.com/*) focuses on deep .NET and Java support and integration for enterprise PaaS adoption behind the firewall. It helps with adding SaaS enablement to regular .NET and Java applications.

CloudBees: portable, managed, public and private cloud

CloudBees (*http://www.cloudbees.com/*) started as a Java-only PaaS that incorporated common tools used within Java platforms. It has since expanded to support many more languages including Node.js, Go, and Erlang and others. CloudBees also has fantastic Jenkins integration for continuous integration.

Cloud Foundry: portable, unmanaged, public and private cloud

Cloud Foundry (*http://www.cloudfoundry.com/use*) offers a set of more than a dozen programs that are loosely coupled and work together to provide PaaS functionality.

DotCloud: portable, managed, public cloud

DotCloud (*https://www.dotcloud.com/*) was the first PaaS to support multiple languages and technologies. It supports Ruby, Node.js, Python, PHP, and Java.

EngineYard: portable, managed, public cloud

EngineYard (*http://www.engineyard.com/*) was one of the first PaaS companies and has thousands of production customers. It supports Ruby, PHP, and Node. Developers get full root access to their dedicated virtual servers and the flexibility of custom Chef recipes to control and automate their entire environment, regardless of size. EngineYard's highly regarded DevOps and support team has expertise in application analysis, code and security audits, custom Chef, deployment, scaling, and high availability strategies.

Force.com: non-portable, managed, public cloud

Force.com (*http://www.force.com/*) is SalesForce's proprietary PaaS for accessing SalesForce data directly. It has been able to create an ecosystem of applications around CRM data.

Google App Engine: semi-portable, managed, public cloud

Google App Engine (*https://developers.google.com/appengine/*) was one of the very earliest forms of PaaS, with a large following and a large developer mindshare behind it. Its promise to take advantage of the power of Google has helped to make it a leader in PaaS.

Google App Engine started out as a non-portable PaaS but is moving toward portability and can even run WordPress applications with the addition of PHP support.

Heroku: portable, managed, public cloud

Heroku (*http://www.heroku.com/*) was one of the first cloud platforms. It supports Ruby, Java, Python, Clojure, Scala, Node.js, and other languages.

Windows Azure: semi-portable, managed, public cloud

Azure (*http://www.windowsazure.com/*) started out as non-portable but has been moving slowly toward portability. Microsoft also provides standard services that can scale independently.

IaaS Providers

When it comes to provisioning virtual servers, IaaS is the fastest way to do it. With IaaS providers, you get dedicated servers with dedicated IP addresses. They start out as a blank slate, so you have to do all the system administration, software installation, tuning, and managing. You can use many of the private-cloud, unmanaged PaaS providers listed in this chapter on many of these providers:

Amazon Web Services

AWS (*http://aws.amazon.com/*) currently is the most popular IaaS in use. Amazon uses Xen to virtualize its infrastructure across more than a dozen availability zones around the world.

DataPipe

DataPipe (*http://datapipe.com/*) offers its own infrastructure, as well as reselling Amazon Web Services with more managed services on top. The extra services include monitoring, patching, change management, deployment, and more.

GoGrid

GoGrid (*http://www.gogrid.com/*) is a high-performance IaaS managed hosting provider.

Google Compute Engine

Google (*http://cloud.google.com/products/compute-engine.html*) has built its IaaS service to compete with Amazon and others. The performance is significantly higher than Amazon's at the same price point.

HP Cloud Services

HP Cloud (*http://hpcloud.com/*) is a relatively new IaaS offering in the market. It is a public cloud built on OpenStack technology running in various HP data centers around the world.

Joyent

Joyent (*http://joyent.com/*) is an IaaS provider targeting large enterprises. Instead of virtualizing the OS like most traditional IaaS providers, Joyent uses its SmartOS technology (based on Solaris), which combines ZFS, DTrace, Zones, and KVM and has better performance characteristics than traditional virtualization.

OpenStack

OpenStack (*http://www.openstack.org/*) is an open source library made up of various components that aims to simulate the API experience of IaaS providers like AWS.

The components of OpenStack currently include:

- Compute (*https://github.com/openstack/nova*) (code name Nova)
- Object Storage (*https://github.com/openstack/swift*) (code name Swift)
- Block Storage (*https://github.com/openstack/cinder*) (code name Cinder)
- Networking (*https://github.com/openstack/quantum*) (code name Quantum)
- Dashboard (*https://github.com/openstack/horizon*) (code name Horizon)
- Identity Services (*https://github.com/openstack/keystone*) (code name Keystone)
- Image Services (*https://github.com/openstack/glance*) (code name Glance)

Rackspace

Rackspace (*http://www.rackspace.com/*) is a provider of fanatical support for managed hosting of both Linux and Windows. Rackspace worked with NASA to originally sponsor the OpenStack project and has incorporated OpenStack to run its public cloud IaaS today.

Savvis

Savvis (*http://www.savvis.com/*) (now owned by CenturyLink) is a large enterprise–focused provider of VMware-based public cloud IaaS with the option of managed services. The servers run by Savvis can be completely managed and software upgraded by Savvis if you like.

TerreMark

TerreMark (*http://www.terremark.com/*) (now owned by Verizon) is another large enterprise–focused VMware-based public cloud IaaS that is sold in blocks of resources as opposed to virtual machine instances.

Windows Azure

Although Azure (*http://www.windowsazure.com/*) started out as a PaaS application, it has expanded into IaaS capabilities. The Windows support is fantastic, and it even has support for Linux. However, the Linux support is currently limited to 20 virtual machines within a subnet, so it may not be as scalable as other providers in this list for Linux.

Managed Services

When approaching managed services, it's critical that you plan ahead. Think about how to approach and get past the scalability limits of any particular service. As long as you have thought through these scenarios, starting with a managed service will always be faster than setting it up for yourself. The following sections list some of the options.

Data storage: MySQL

- ClearDB (*http://www.cleardb.com/*)
- Amazon RDS (*http://aws.amazon.com/rds/*)

Data storage: PostgreSQL

- Heroku Postgres (*https://postgres.heroku.com/*)

Data storage: CouchDB

- IrisCouch (*http://www.iriscouch.com/*)

Data storage: MongoDB

- MongoLab (*https://mongolab.com/*)
- MongoHQ (*https://www.mongohq.com/*)

Data storage: NoSQL

- Cloudant (*https://cloudant.com/*)
- Neo4j (*http://www.neo4j.org/*)

Data storage: Redis

- Redis To Go (*http://redistogo.com/*)
- OpenRedis (*https://openredis.com/*)
- Redis Cloud (*http://redis-cloud.com/*)

Data storage: Caching

- MemCachier (*https://www.memcachier.com/*)
- IronCache (*http://www.iron.io/cache*)

Mobile

- Urban Airship (*http://urbanairship.com/*)
- Pusher (*http://pusher.com/*)
- Realtime.co (*http://www.realtime.co/*)
- PubNub (*http://www.pubnub.com/*)
- Twilio (*http://www.twilio.com/*)

Search

- Searchify (*https://www.searchify.com/*)
- Websolr (*http://www.websolr.com/*)
- AWS CloudSearch (*http://aws.amazon.com/cloudsearch/*)
- Treasure Data (*http://www.treasure-data.com/*)

Logging

- Loggly (*http://loggly.com/*)
- Logentries (*http://logentries.com/*)

- Papertrail (*https://papertrailapp.com/*)

Email

- Mailgun (*http://www.mailgun.com/*)
- Sendgrid (*http://sendgrid.com/*)
- CloudMailin (*http://www.cloudmailin.com/*)

Background Tasks

- IronMQ (*http://www.iron.io/mq*)
- IronWorker (*http://www.iron.io/worker*)
- CloudAMQP (*http://www.cloudamqp.com/*): RabbitMQ-as-a-Service

Analytics

- Statsmix (*http://www.statsmix.com/*)
- NewRelic (*http://newrelic.com/*)
- Blitz (*http://blitz.io/*)

Error Monitoring

- Exceptional (*http://www.exceptional.io/*)
- Airbrake (*https://airbrake.io/pages/home*)

Utilities

- Zerigo (*http://www.zerigo.com/*): DNS
- CloudFlare (*https://www.cloudflare.com/*): CDN + Security + Analytics
- Codeship (*https://www.codeship.io/*): Hosted continuous integration/continuous deployment

Payments

- Recurly (*http://recurly.com/*)

- Stripe (*https://stripe.com/*)
- Spreedly (*https://spreedly.com/*)

Migrating Legacy Apps to PaaS

Legacy applications can come in all flavors, from blogs and content management systems to custom applications written long ago in a forgotten language. Here are a few links to resources for common blog and content management systems that should help you if you need to modernize and make your blog or other apps more cloudy.

WordPress Plug-ins

- UpdraftPlus Backup (*http://wordpress.org/extend/plugins/updraftplus/*)
- CDN Sync Tool (*http://wordpress.org/extend/plugins/cdn-sync-tool/*)
- Amazon S3 Uploads (*http://wordpress.org/extend/plugins/amazon-s3-uploads/*)

Drupal Modules

- Storage API (*http://drupal.org/project/storage_api*)
- Amazon S3 (*http://drupal.org/project/amazon_s3*)
- Cloud Files (*http://drupal.org/project/cloud_files*)
- S3 Auto Pushing (*http://drupal.org/project/s3autopush*)

Joomla! Plug-ins

- JA Amazon S3 (*http://tinyurl.com/ja-amazon-s3*)
- jomCDN (*http://tinyurl.com/jomcdn*)

Greenfield PaaS App Development

When building new applications on PaaS, it is recommended to build them RESTfully. There are frameworks well suited to quickly generating RESTful applications in every language you can think of. Here are a few selected popular choices—there are many quality options not listed here, but this should get you started.

Ruby

- Ruby on Rails (*http://rubyonrails.org/*)
- Sinatra (*http://www.sinatrarb.com/*)
- RESTRack (*http://restrack.me/*)

Python

- Django REST Framework (*http://django-rest-framework.org/*)
- Flask (*http://flask.pocoo.org/*)
- Bottle (*http://bottlepy.org/*)

Node.js

- Express (*http://expressjs.com/*)
- Tower (*http://towerjs.org/*)
- Restify (*http://mcavage.github.com/node-restify/*)

PHP

- Slim (*http://www.slimframework.com/*)
- Recess (*http://www.recessframework.org/*)
- Tonic (*http://peej.github.com/tonic/*)

Java

- Restlet (*http://www.restlet.org/*)
- Jersey (*http://jersey.java.net/*)
- Spring (*http://www.springsource.org/*)

.NET

- OpenRasta (*http://openrasta.org/*)
- WCF (*http://msdn.microsoft.com/en-us/library/dd456779.aspx*)

- RESTful .NET (*http://shop.oreilly.com/product/9780596519216.do*) (O'Reilly)

Perl

- Mojolicious (*http://mojolicio.us/*)
- Dancer (*http://perldancer.org/*)
- Catalyst (*http://www.catalystframework.org/*)

Index

We'd like to hear your suggestions for improving our indexes. Send email to index@oreilly.com.

O

object storage, 40–44
Objective-C language, 74
open source
    about, 10, 35
    closed source comparison, 97
    limitations of, 109
    regaining control through, 108
    resources for, 109
OpenShift tool, 10, 35, 97
OpenStack library, 105, 107, 114
operating expense (opex), 17
optimization development trap, 55
outages, handling, 107

P

PaaS (Platform-as-a-Service)
    benefits of, 10, 18–23, 34, 49, 68, 102
    cloud technology and, 3, 7–8
    core services, 81–93
    developer considerations, 2
    future of, 11, 105
    greenfield apps, 33
    IaaS comparison, 21, 105
    language considerations, 8, 20, 22
    legacy apps, 33, 37–56
    limitations of, 98–101, 102–103
    managed versus productized platforms, 10
    mobile apps on, 71–79
    non-portable, 25–28, 33, 111
    open source, 35
    portable, 28–33, 79, 111
    provider listing, 111–113
    situations not advantageous to, 95–103
    types of, 25–36
    writing apps for, 57–70
PHP language
    Amazon S3 and, 41
    caching considerations, 49
    session management and, 46
planning upgrade paths, 91–93
Platform-as-a-Service (see PaaS)
plug-ins (CMS), 44
portable PaaS, 28–33, 79, 111
POST command, 63
PostgreSQL databasese, 49
private cloud
    about, 10, 95, 112

enterprises and, 98
open and closed source options, 97
public cloud versus, 95
small- and medium-sized businesses, 96
productized platforms, 10
programming languages, 48
    (see also specific languages)
    caching techniques and, 48
    PaaS considerations, 8, 20, 22
public cloud
    about, 10, 111
    distributed systems and, 59
    email providers and, 87
    enterprises and, 97
    OpenStack and, 105
    private cloud versus, 95
    small- and medium-sized businesses, 96
Puppet tool, 5
PUT command, 62

Q

queries (SQL), 83

R

Rackspace Cloud Files, 43, 105, 114
Redis key/value store, 50
redundancy in caches, 87
Representational State Transfer (REST), 61, 78
resources
    greenfield app development, 118
    IaaS providers, 113–115
    managed services, 115–117
    moving legacy apps, 118
    open source, 109
    PaaS providers, 111–113
Resque project, 52
REST (Representational State Transfer), 61, 78
REST API, 30, 79, 108
RESTful metaservices, 65–67
RestKit framework, 75
Restlet library, 78
RightScale tool, 5
Ruby language
    ActiveResource library, 65
    caching considerations, 50
    Rackspace Cloud Files and, 43
    scheduling background tasks, 52
    session management and, 47

About the Author

Lucas Carlson founded AppFog, a PaaS company that leveraged Cloud Foundry and was acquired by CenturyLink in 2013. Lucas has been a professional developer for 10 years and specializes in Ruby on Rails development. Lucas has authored *Programming for PaaS*, coauthored the *Ruby Cookbook*, and has written half a dozen libraries in various programming languages and contributed to many others, including Rails and RedCloth. He maintains a personal website at rufy.com (*http://rufy.com/*).

Colophon

The animal on the cover of *Programming for PaaS* is the common hare (belonging to the genus *Lepus*), which is a larger, more athletic relative of the rabbit. Hares are able to adapt to a variety of habitats and so are some of the most widely distributed land animals in the world (although they are most commonly found in Europe and North America).

The hare is one of the fastest of all the smaller animals, being able to move at speeds of around 45 miles per hour. The strong hind legs of the hare, combined with its large feet, give it the ability to run so quickly. The hare is also able to jump over large distances with great ease. It is primarily herbivorous and eats grasses, herbs, and field crops.

Normally shy animals, hares change their behavior in spring, when they can be seen in broad daylight chasing one another around meadows; this appears to be competition between males to attain dominance (and hence more access to breeding females). During this spring frenzy, hares can be seen "boxing": one hare strikes another with its paws.

Hares have often been used as symbolic signs—the definitions of which differ between cultures—and they are also some of the most common animals used in folklore and stories. The hare is often associated with moon deities and signifies rebirth and resurrection. It is a symbol of fertility, sensuality, and serves as an attribute for hunting.

The cover image is from Cassell's *Natural History*. The cover font is Adobe ITC Garamond. The text font is Adobe Minion Pro; the heading font is Adobe Myriad Condensed; and the code font is Dalton Maag's Ubuntu Mono.

Get even more for your money.

Join the O'Reilly Community, and register the O'Reilly books you own. It's free, and you'll get:

- $4.99 ebook upgrade offer
- 40% upgrade offer on O'Reilly print books
- Membership discounts on books and events
- Free lifetime updates to ebooks and videos
- Multiple ebook formats, DRM FREE
- Participation in the O'Reilly community
- Newsletters
- Account management
- 100% Satisfaction Guarantee

Signing up is easy:

1. Go to: oreilly.com/go/register
2. Create an O'Reilly login.
3. Provide your address.
4. Register your books.

Note: English-language books only

To order books online:
oreilly.com/store

For questions about products or an order:
orders@oreilly.com

To sign up to get topic-specific email announcements and/or news about upcoming books, conferences, special offers, and new technologies:
elists@oreilly.com

For technical questions about book content:
booktech@oreilly.com

To submit new book proposals to our editors:
proposals@oreilly.com

O'Reilly books are available in multiple DRM-free ebook formats. For more information:
oreilly.com/ebooks

O'REILLY®

Spreading the knowledge of innovators   oreilly.com

Milton Keynes UK
Ingram Content Group UK Ltd.
UKHW010755280724
446142UK00007B/116